Praise for *Love the Home You Have*

Melissa Michaels, how did you get into my every house-obsessed thought? Anyone who has long balanced visions (yes, plural) of dream houses (plural again) with fickle dissatisfaction for a current abode, will find themselves in *Love the Home You Have*. Threaded with stories of this beloved blogger's life journey through six houses—and lessons learned from each—this guidebook coaches those who love architecture, decorating, and design to acknowledge that we can live with imperfection because we care about contentment far more. When you print the "I Brake for Charming Houses" bumper sticker, I'll take one.

—Jill Waage, Executive Editor, Better Homes and Gardens Brand

Melissa's *Love the Home You Have* is charming, witty, and gracious. She gets to the heart of joyful living by sharing the importance of vulnerability, authenticity, and honesty within ourselves. Melissa gives all of us Pinterest lovers (yes, that's me!) the freedom to let our homes evolve day-to-day, season-to-season. Her encouragement to be authentic by inviting others in, no matter the state or the style of our homes, is soothing advice for those reluctant to practice hospitality and mirrors a beautiful message to guests that "their authenticity is in style, too!"

—Sandy Coughlin, author and founder of
ReluctantEntertainer.com

Melissa Michaels offers the cure to comparison every woman needs: contentment. She'll inspire you to have a home that's not only lovely but a true reflection of what matters most to you and a haven for those you love. It's time to let go of the pressure and expectations you've always felt so you can fully discover and embrace the beauty of the space where you are right now.

—Holley Gerth, *Wall Street Journal* bestselling author of
You're Already Amazing

For years, Melissa's words have encouraged me to push aside unrealistic expectations in my home and celebrate authentic living. *Love the Home You Have* does that and more. Melissa's nurturing heart celebrates what a well lived home is all about and gives us permission to start creating our dream home right where we are at. What an inspiring read! Our home is so much more than their walls. With her help, we can make it a true haven.

—Jen Schmidt, creator of the blog Balancing Beauty and Bedlam, co-founder of the Becoming Conference

Melissa's thoughtful call to contentment comes complete with helpful tips and action items, but more than anything it gives us permission to embrace imperfections and soak up the goodness of the Lord no matter where He leads us to live. What a much-needed reminder that home functions best when it's a sanctuary, not a showroom.

—Sophie Hudson, author of *Home Is Where My People Are* and blogger at BooMama.net

I've always believed God has us where we are for a reason. He doesn't waste a thing—including the fixer-upper seasons of life. This lovely book is your guide to falling in love with your home, no matter its size or condition. From the whimsical illustrations to the practical suggestions, you will love Melissa's encouragement to love the home you have.

—Kristen Welch, author of *Rhinestone Jesus*

LOVE the HOME you HAVE

MELISSA MICHAELS

HARVEST HOUSE PUBLISHERS
EUGENE, OREGON

Scripture quotations are taken from the New American Standard Bible®, © 1960, 1962, 1963, 1968, 1971, 1972, 1973, 1975, 1977, 1995 by The Lockman Foundation. Used by permission. (www.Lockman.org)

Cover and Interior Design by Harvest House Publishers, Inc., Eugene, Oregon

Published in association with William K. Jensen Literary Agency, 119 Bampton Court, Eugene, Oregon 97404.

Love the Home You Have
Copyright © 2015 Melissa Michaels
Published by Harvest House Publishers
Eugene, Oregon 97402
www.harvesthousepublishers.com

Library of Congress Cataloging-in-Publication Data

Michaels, Melissa,
 Love the home you have / Melissa Michaels.
  pages cm
 ISBN 978-0-7369-6307-7 (pbk.)
 ISBN 978-0-7369-6308-4 (eBook)
 1. Interior decoration. 2. Domestic space. I. Title.
 NK2115.M46 2015
 747—dc23

2014035605

Printed in the United States of America

15 16 17 18 19 20 21 22 23 / VB-KBD / 10 9 8 7 6 5 4 3 2 1

Contents

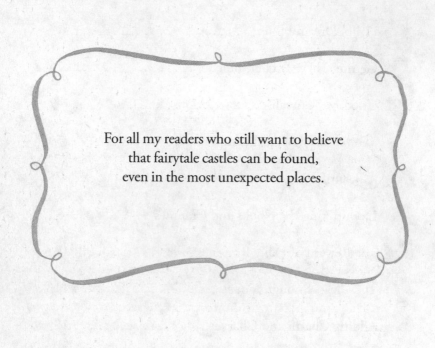

For all my readers who still want to believe
that fairytale castles can be found,
even in the most unexpected places.

Home Is in the Heart of the Beholder

We tend to forget that happiness doesn't come as a result of getting something we don't have, but rather of recognizing and appreciating what we do have.
FREDERICK KEONIG

I've been a house lover from as far back as I can remember. Creating beauty in a home is a little bit of heaven for me. I enjoy the simple daily rituals of keeping house. I love to light nice-smelling candles. I have fun puttering around, rearranging accessories and even furniture on a regular basis. I get giddy over polished white sinks and clean counters. I regularly stop to appreciate little things around my home—how pretty my bed looks after I make it, the way the sun filters softly through my windows, how the colors of my walls flow nicely from room to room.

I take pleasure in seeing seasonal decor on my porch, pretty dishes stacked on my open kitchen shelves, and organized baskets and glass jars in my pantry. Honestly, I fall in love with my home a little bit more every day. I can imagine being content here for the rest of my life!

And *that*, my friend, is what I've discovered throughout my journey. The attitude of contentment was a life lesson I have learned over time and am still learning. And it's the heart of this journey we are starting together.

The Big Discovery

I spent many years convinced my own dream house was the one found beyond the picket fence or behind the big iron gates. It was the one near the water or the one down the block. The big one. The small one. The charming cottage on the corner.

I tried them all, and each time I was certain it was THE ONE.

Only to find it wasn't the *only* one.

The dream house is here too, under this new roof of the only house I didn't dream of or fall in love with or even consider our forever home. It's here in the place I hang clothes and chase dust bunnies and bake cookies and wipe the muddy paws of puppies. The place I rearrange furniture and hang curtains and burn the toast.

The most important thing I've learned from all my dreaming, scheming, and hauling moving boxes is that we can learn to love the

home we have whether it is big or small, fancy or ordinary, surrounded by white pickets or brown chain link, faced with brick or faux siding, a first apartment or a starter home in a less-than-ideal neighborhood.

Home is right where you are.

As for those dreams you have about what a home should look like? They can come alive wherever you are, in any size, shape, or style of house, with all of its limitations and frustrations, once you embrace who you really are, what you love, and your own authentic style at home.

I won't try to persuade you to create a house that looks just like mine. All of our dream houses look a little bit different. This book isn't about learning to transform your home by becoming a DIY expert (unless you want to be one) or a Martha Stewart clone (unless you have a big staff). It isn't about lowering the bar of your expectations. (I think we find hope and contentment when we dream big with realistic passion!) My goal is to offer you inspiration and confidence so you can create a dream house, whatever that looks like to you. We are all unique. We all have different styles. We all have different limitations. But the formula for a house you love should work just as well whether you move to a new address or settle in and embrace the one you already have.

Fresh Beginnings Are Life's Little Remodels

Start today. You don't have to take out a loan, trade in your husband or kids (even if you're tempted to), or win the lottery before you begin. The exciting result of learning to love the home you have is this: You will find greater contentment where you are, and your home will start to inspire your life in unexpected ways.

Each of us is coming from a different place. Some women are single and living on their own, others are newly married, and still others are living in the chaos of having young kids and pets and hectic jobs. You and I might have different lives, but our shared truth is that the scenery and demands of our lives are always changing. The kind of home projects we take on or the updates we make will vary with the season we are in. Once we start working within our limitations rather than wishing them away, we are making forward motion toward living a contented life at home. Here are three ways to jump-start your journey:

1. List three reasons you're grateful for the home you have.

2. Start a special tradition or create a fun memory in your home.

3. Think of one area of your home you enjoy and why.

I'm here to encourage you through my own home stories and the lessons I've learned so you can confidently take the next step, embrace authenticity in the journey, and even delight in the unexpected twists and turns that contribute to your dream of a beautiful home and life. Right there in the home you have.

The Love Your Home Challenge

Have you ever walked into a home and right away sensed a special heart-and-soul warmth? When you engage your own personal style to transform your life within your four walls, your house becomes that kind of home. The place you live should feel like your own little 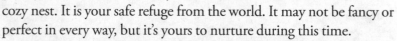 cozy nest. It is your safe refuge from the world. It may not be fancy or perfect in every way, but it's yours to nurture during this time.

The memories, the love, and the personal touches we put into our home will transform it from a basic structure to a place that actually enhances our life. The more we invest our self in each corner of our home, the more emotionally connected we become.

To inspire you in that direction, I'm inviting you to take the 31-Day Love Your Home Challenge. You'll find this as a special section following chapter 13. You can use the challenge as you journey with me or after you've read the book as a way to begin using the ideas and encouragement you gather along the way. Honestly, real love doesn't always start with a feeling, but with actions that eventually result in feelings.

Go ahead and take a peek at it right now! I'll wait for you. Think about how you want to make the most of the challenge and its encouraging, useful prompts.

Love the Home You Have Online

To make this home-love journey as simple as possible, I want you to have a clear starting place to connect with me and find encouragement long after you turn the last page of this book. Besides reading and subscribing to my blog at theinspiredroom.net, I've created a special online home just for you and other readers of this book.

At lovethehomeyouhave.com you'll find links to helpful articles I've written, downloads of the printable art, quotations and resources you will find listed in this book, and a link to a special Pinterest board I set up for inspiration and support related to this book experience and your home-love journey.

Share the Love

Throughout this book you will come across some happy hand-drawn quotations—words of encouragement created for you to enjoy. When you get to these, I hope you'll pause and take in these messages of hope. You might even find the perfect one to be your special "I love my home" motto.

Feel free to snap a pic of any of these and post, Pin, or Tweet them (#lovethehomeyouhave) to encourage friends. As a gift to you, I've also placed the entire selection of quotations online at lovethehomeyouhave.com as free downloadable prints you can use and share as much as you like. Feel free to print one that really fits your mood, your life, or your home-love status and keep it handy as your reminder to dream big, embrace what you have, and appreciate the incredible combination of mess and beauty that is your home.

At this site, you'll also find a personal invitation to discover fun ways to share your own journey with me and other readers through becoming a part of my new interactive site called Home Love Stories (homelovestories.com). We'll celebrate this journey together as we open up about our 31-Day Challenge experiences, share our personal home stories, and upload photos, ideas, failures, and successes. Let's make this a great community. I can't wait to see you there!

So let's begin! And may this adventure inspire your love for the home you have.

CHAPTER 1

Hello, Dream House

*When you finally go back to your old home, you'll find it
wasn't the old home you missed but your childhood.*
SAM EWING

I've always been a bit of a romantic. As a young girl, I was full of
fanciful ideas about life, love, and creating a home. I imagined a
fairy-tale, happily-ever-after version of life full of pretty things and
extraordinary moments on ordinary Mondays. The chance to create
a lovely home and a beautiful life is the one true dream I have been
passionate about since my earliest memories.

My favorite thing to do as a kid (besides playing with my Barbie
dream house and wallpapering the walls of cardboard-box dollhouses)
was to ride in the backseat of my parents' car for our Sunday afternoon
drive-bys. We'd quietly drive up the winding driveways of the most
amazing houses, past the Beware of Dog signs and security cameras,
and peer through the gates to catch glimpses of the glories on the other
side.

Be still my heart. I thought those beautiful homes were as majes-
tic as fairy-tale castles. They were what my dreams were made of. I
imagined that someday, somehow, I would live in a big, fancy English
Tudor.

I think many of us have mental images of what life is supposed to
look like. Maybe you didn't grow up thinking you were going to be a

princess living in an English castle, but I bet you had your own version of what your grown-up world would look like.

> *I am a grown-up, and somewhere along the line I stopped going into that place in my own mind where grace and casual elegance lived. Things around here are in a dismal state of affairs. Really, my life is a little past the halfway mark, and I would truly like to live some of it the way I imagined it as a little girl. You have spurred me on to reach into my past and all the dreams and wonders of how it would be when I became a grown-up.*
>
> *—an Inspired Room blog reader*

Perhaps your dream was planted in your mind when you were just a little girl, or maybe the ideal has been budding more recently. It may be fueled by visual tours of picture-perfect lives on Instagram, where everyone else seems to have a beautiful home with well-placed bouquets on lovely tables and no dirty laundry anywhere (unless it is actually clean and color-coordinated and then strewn about to give the space an artistic, lived-in look). Of course, we know the images are staged and filtered so the homes appear to be perfect, but still…we can't help but dream about having a home that beautiful.

There is a reason Instagram is addictive—it's inspiring to look at. Who in their right mind wants to see pictures of anyone's dirty laundry on the floor? No one. We don't crave ugly or disorganized things. We want pretty. We want organized. We love to dream a little. Is that too much to ask?

Why We Long for Beauty

Where does our desire for a lovely or orderly home come from? Is it an unhealthy obsession with perfection? Not necessarily. The question is, are we experiencing the joy of creating a beautiful atmosphere at home, or are we fostering discontent by obsessing over what we don't

The Five Gifts of Change

1. *Change creates a new beginning.* Yesterday may have been about tears, dissatisfaction, and letting go, but today is different. Change of any kind gives birth to a new beginning. Embrace the possibility with gusto.

2. *Change shifts things.* This adventure sets you on a new path and gives you a fresh vantage point. Today you are blessed with the chance to look at your life and home from a new perspective.

3. *Change calls you to action.* I have always felt that God wants to use people who are willing to move their feet. You will definitely get moving in this pursuit of a newfound love for your home. Each change you encounter will encourage and enlighten you as you walk through the next one.

4. *Change ignites your imagination.* This journey you begin today will spark your creativity. Ask yourself, "What if? What if I traded my dark curtains for light linen panels? What if I turned my dining room into my office? What if I believed in transformation?" Creativity makes dreams come true.

5. *Change inspires confidence.* If you doubt your talent or sense of style, make a list of your passions and move forward with hope. Trade your fear of failure for the joy of trying. Whether you are redesigning a room or redesigning your life, you can do it with confidence.

have? We can't control everything life throws our way, but we can learn to beautify and manage our home.

In truth, we long to do this—and not because we are greedy. It's quite the opposite. We nurture our love of beauty and order in our homes because we are grateful.

Has one of God's brilliant sunrises ever taken your breath away? Has your heart nearly leapt out of your chest at the sight of a newborn baby and the miracle of new life? Creation isn't filled with wonder by accident—I believe it was intricately designed. And we are attracted to it with all our being. God placed the desire for order and beauty within us, and we feel a connection to it the moment we witness it.

Our longing to be surrounded by beauty isn't frivolous or unrealistic. It helps us turn our houses into homes and our someday-dreams into our realities. The lifelong opportunity to create and appreciate beauty all around us is a gift we are granted by God. We are blessed to manage our own little heaven on earth—our homes—wherever they might be.

There is divine purpose in caring for our homes and wanting them to be places of loveliness and peace. Our homes won't ever be perfect, but we certainly can enjoy the process of creating beauty, and we can appreciate the lessons we learn along the way. There's hope for house lovers and beauty seekers regardless of the current condition of our surroundings. We need only to grab ahold of our dreams right where we are in the everyday, beautiful mess of real life.

Dream-House Stalkers, Unite!

After many years of adulthood and supposed maturity, I'm still stalking beautiful houses, just as I did when I was a kid staring out the backseat window of our family car. But now I'm the one at the wheel, maneuvering around my favorite neighborhoods. I look at houses differently now than I did as a kid. My glance through a wrought-iron gate at someone else's beautiful home doesn't send me into fantasy mode. Instead, it nudges me to stop daydreaming about what I don't have and to start falling in love with what I do have.

A favorite pastime of mine is to venture out at night to look at houses in the dark, when the interior lights are on, so I can get a glimpse of how cute they are inside. The rooms, I mean, *not* the people in the homes. I don't even look at the people, I promise. Maybe house stalking is an addiction. (I can't seem to stop. Do I need a treatment program?) Or maybe it is an extreme fascination. That's it—I'm a house paparazzi!

I might be in denial, but I like to put a positive spin on these outings by thinking of them as mini business trips for my blog. (Now you know why bloggers might seem a bit insane at times. We've turned our addictions into careers, and we call them our passions. But that's another book.)

I actually prefer to do a walk-by of my favorite houses so I can get closer with my zoom lens when I want to get a picture of someone's beautiful gate or front door. I know, it sounds weird and borderline illegal to take photos of people's front doors. Believe me, this behavior has scared my husband once or twice. One minute I'm standing outside the car, and the next minute I've disappeared from his rearview mirror. He probably fears I've climbed over a fence and fallen prey to an angry guard dog or been apprehended by the neighborhood patrol. I'm happy to report that neither of these scenarios have happened…yet.

My dream-house stalking adventures might seem risky, but I try to respect the law and neighborhood rules. And as a good citizen, I will even drive by twice just to keep the traffic flowing (and because impatient drivers in the cars behind me keep trying to rush me). Not everyone appreciates my love of houses, so I politely (or loudly under my breath from inside my car) let them know I have important business to attend to in the neighborhood. I really need a bumper sticker that says, "I brake for charming houses." Then drivers behind me would know to expect my sudden stops and swerves, and they could drive accordingly.

One day during our first year in our current neighborhood, I went on a walk. I wasn't expecting to see anything particularly noteworthy, so I was delighted when I came upon a house so charming it stopped me in my tracks. At first I felt a little sad that my house wasn't as nice,

and a bit of envy started to well up inside of me. But when I got closer, I noticed something wonderful. It *was* like my house, at least on the outside. Only it was more finished with details, like landscaping and trellises. I now had a fresh vision for my own home.

Similarly, a couple of years ago I attended a few open houses along the water near me. While I was mid-grumble about how the grass is always greener, I looked at these model homes and realized I loved them because they had freshly painted walls and trim. All mine needed was paint! That I could do, and I didn't even have to move or spend $100,000 more to live the dream. (Okay, so my house isn't along the waterfront, but we do have a slight view of the water from our upstairs bathroom. You take what you can get, right?)

Falling in love with the home I have often starts with studying a room or home or style I love. Once I realize what I love about it, I'm able to figure out how to get that same feeling in my home and on my budget. There is always a personal takeaway when scouting for inspiration. And that's just what I tell the neighborhood patrol when I'm on drive-bys. It's part of my education. I'm a harmless, house-stalking, beautiful-room-loving dreamer.

It's what I do. It's who I am.

If friends happen to have a lovely house and invite me over, things can get awkward. I am easily distracted by shiny things—like their newly remodeled kitchen. As they tell me about their summer vacation, my eyes might dart to the right as I strain to look at their choice of cabinet hardware. Nothing says, "I'm listening," quite like someone's eyes drifting in another direction, right?

But honestly, instead of being jealous or depressed when I'm drooling over my neighbor's new sink and faucet, I actually find artistic inspiration in beautiful homes. Studying why I love beautiful things challenges me to see them as works of art and not as impossible dreams. I enjoy beauty simply because it's beautiful and because it inspires me to recreate it in my own way, in my own four walls, and within my ability and means.

We may not be able to afford other people's expensive houses, but that doesn't mean we can't learn a thing or two from them that we can apply to our own, perhaps more humble, homes. And if you have a sprawling home, it might be the cozy cottage downtown that gets you a wee bit jealous. You can still gather ideas about adding charm and making good use of space in your bigger house. Have you ever thought about changing how you view a beautiful house? Perhaps instead of being envious, you could find a way to be inspired!

Develop a Crush on Your Home

It might seem very backward to begin falling in love with your home by first coveting the cove ceilings of a friend's entryway. Perhaps it seems like a recipe for discontentment and unhappiness. But trust me, as you gather ideas and learn to appreciate beauty, you will discover the qualities, characteristics, and styles that are most appealing to you. It's about identifying the tangible and intangible special features that light up your eyes. It's about sparking a bit of a crush on your home by ultimately turning your attention and wish list back to it and saying, "I know just the TLC you need."

So let's begin here. Go ahead and dream with me for a little bit. What does your dream house look like? It's okay to dig down deep to remember what you once believed a beautiful home would look like.

Do you know what kind of home you love, or are you still trying to figure that out? You might discover your dream house on a blog or Pinterest or in a magazine. Maybe you've seen a home you love in person, and you decide to risk life and limb for a closer view, just as I do. Take your camera with you on walks so you can capture inspiration in the moment. Create lists of what you see that you like or don't like. Save your dream-house pictures on Pinterest, or go old-school and rip them out of magazines to create an inspiration board or notebook.

As you dream, you'll start to get an idea of what you love and want for your own home. Don't worry if it's beyond your means or it looks nothing like the house you have now. What's most important is that you can see it in your mind even if you can't see it when you open your eyes. We can deal with reality later…and it will be fun.

—Style Notes—

Putting your ideal decorating style into words helps clarify your vision for what you want your home to look and feel like. Learning to *describe* what you love now will help you make decisions later. So…what's your favorite style? Feel free to make up words!

Keep On Dreaming

Keep dreaming until you can picture the whole house—front to back and every room in between. Even if you have your doubts that you'll ever live in such a home, stick with it. Let yourself enjoy dreaming.

DREAM BIG! I'll wait until you're done...

Now that you've established the dream, open your eyes. How far off the mark is your life at home right now? If it's way off, don't panic or run for cover in your bed and console yourself with a bowlful of ice cream and hot fudge just yet.

I believe you can live your dream wherever you are. Yes, in *that* house. The one you saw when you opened your eyes. The one with the piles of clutter or undecorated rooms or mismatched hand-me-down furniture or empty walls. The too-small house with maroon carpet. The house that needs more windows or closets or bedrooms. The one that keeps you too busy with endless repairs and cleaning. The one you don't want to call your forever home.

And no, I'm not crazy. At least I don't think so. I like to think of myself as creatively optimistic. Where there's a will, there's a way—no matter what the obstacle. I believe you can cultivate a love for your home regardless of your current circumstances or limitations. You just have to take the first step.

Loving the home you have isn't about settling for what makes you unhappy or pining away, coveting something you don't have. In fact, neither of those choices will lead to contentment at all.

Our obstacles and limitations are actually opportunities to create something more beautiful. As we redesign our homes, we start to feel more alive and in touch with the people we were created to be. We can put our own stamp of beauty right where we are when we look beyond our homes as they are to what they could be.

Beauty and Bliss

The desire to transform our everyday experience empowers us to live a full and meaningful and contented life. And the God who created you and the beauty outside your front door will delight in being reflected throughout your home.

Is the grass really greener on the other side of the fence? No. The grass is greener where you water it. When dreamers and house lovers learn to find contentment right where they are, wonderful things start to happen. Our homes become places that inspire and change the world around us.

I happen to love a good challenge. The house you have may look nothing like your dream house. Or maybe it's close to the dream already but you've lost that lovin' feeling—your zeal for homemaking. Either way, we're going to have fun creating a home you'll love right where you are. I'm excited to be able to help you on this journey, so thanks for letting me come along!

Are you ready to fall in love with the home you have?

Let's Dream

What kind of personality does your dream house have? *Reserved and classy? Happy or serious? Or a mixture of them all?*

What is the style of your dream house, and where is it located? *Tell me more about it—is it a farmhouse? A home on the lake? A mountain lodge? A cottage in a small town? A stylish loft in the city? A spacious, traditional home in the suburbs?*

Describe how well-maintained, clean, or organized it is. *We all have different levels of order and quality that make us happy at home, so consider how important these elements are to you.*

What is your favorite room in your dream house? Why?

What colors draw you in and inspire you?

Do you dream of hosting big formal parties or casual get-togethers in your house?

How would your dream house be a blessing to your family and friends? *Do you dream of entertaining overnight guests or drinking coffee in a cozy room with your best friend?*

What gifts and talents would you like to use in your home? *Do you want to have room for a hobby? Do you dream of running a home business?*

What about a garden? *Do you picture a flower garden or a vegetable garden or a simple landscape?*

CHAPTER 2

Getting There Is Half the Fun

*Optimist: Someone who figures that taking a step backward
after taking a step forward is not a disaster, it's a cha-cha.*
ROBERT BRAULT

Even though I drive by pretty houses purely for fun, part of me
has actually always believed there was a perfect house for me
somewhere. I guess imagining an ideal home was ingrained in
me early on—my childhood hobby was drawing floor plans!

In my Goldilocks mindset, I believed that life would be just right if
only we had more bedrooms so we could spread out all of our stuff, if
only our house was smaller and we could make financial ends meet, if
only I had the magic number of closets and drawers and could be
organized, if only I could find the ideal property, if only I had the right
income to support it all, if only I could find the *perfect* house…then
everything would fall into place and I would live happily ever after.

That's not asking too much, right?

Obviously, my expectations for a perfect home were a bit unrealistic
at times. My crazy dream-house confessions might be different from
your experience, but chances are that you and I both have plenty of
DIY fails and times when our quest for perfection caused more frustration than joy.

In spite of all that, I do know one thing: You and I can both discover
contentment in the same place and at the same time. That would be
right here, right now.

The Fairytale Cottage
{1990-1994}

The English Cottage
{1998-2004}

Home Sweet Home
{2009-Present}

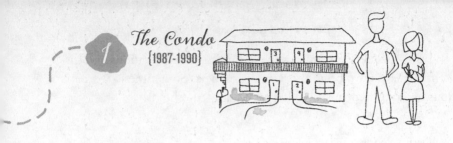

The Condo
{1987-1990}

1

The Picket Fence House
{1994-1998}

3

5

The Castle
{2004-2009}

My Daughter's Townhouse

I truly believe that my seasons of unrealistic expectations and discontentment have been my greatest teachers. Sometimes a woman's journey to contentment is filled with many thresholds.

Newlywed Condo

Jerry and I started out our young-married life in an average, two-bedroom condo. Prior to being a newlywed, I had awakened every morning in a dream house with beautiful sparkles dancing across the ceiling—reflections from the lake that surrounded my family home on three sides. Don't hate me, but that's where I grew up. By comparison, our condominium with its dingy popcorn-textured ceiling and no view lacked the dazzle factor.

As we carried our boxed-up belongings across the threshold of our

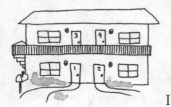

new home, Jerry mentioned with a little laugh that this would probably be the nicest place we would ever live. Say what? I gave him the deer-in-the-headlights look. But he wasn't kidding. He was a realist. I was the dreamer, which is why it hadn't occurred to me that by marrying a guy in ministry, I was agreeing to live in homes that differed ever so slightly from the houses I dreamed about.

I smiled at Jerry and nodded, and we unpacked a few more boxes in awkward silence. His comment opened my eyes to the compromises that would likely come with true love and marital bliss. I fought back a few tears as I took a deep breath and said goodbye to my old house. Our new life together was just beginning, and I wanted to be excited about the path ahead.

Once we were settled, it became clear that there was one other thing the condo lacked that my childhood home clearly had—a cleaning fairy. How else could I explain the perpetual mess? For some strange reason we always had stacks of dirty dishes in the sink right next to the empty dishwasher. Why wasn't the cleaning magically taking place each time we were gone?

Bless our hearts. We had a lot to learn.

We acquired essential beginner DIY skills, such as using faux wood-grain contact paper to cover holes on hollow-core doors and White-Out correction fluid to camouflage burn marks on the white laminate counters. We also had plenty of opportunities to practice conflict resolution.

Three Things I Learned from the Condo

1. A clever fix that fools the eye is sometimes all you need to make something better.

2. Marriage is an opportunity to create a uniquely beautiful home together. Don't be stubborn and demand your own way.

3. Shine a humorous light on your failures. You'll enjoy reliving the story so much more later on.

We were the lucky recipients of a heavy, ugly, hand-me-down sleeper sofa. We sat that hideous sofa right in front of the TV because my darling husband liked it that way. But I had a grander vision. I knew our living room would be so much cozier if only the sofa could be angled toward the corner fireplace. Jerry wasn't convinced.

I was patient with the arrangement as long as I could be, but once I entered the nesting phase of our first pregnancy, my hormones took over. One day while Jerry was at school, I screeched, "I can't stand this arrangement one more minute!" and moved that hefty, hideous sleeper sofa all by my pregnant self. Never underestimate the strength of a mother preparing to give birth.

That evening I admired my design-savvy arrangement while I waited nervously for Jerry's return. And to my relief and his surprise, he loved it. High fives! Our first furniture-rearranging conflict was resolved. I can't say taking matters into my own hands was the best approach for all our disagreements from that point on, but it was a satisfying first.

Together in that condo we endured the crazy people upstairs who vacuumed in the middle of the night, and we learned some surprising facts about housekeeping. Dish soap and dishwashing soap are not the same thing—who knew?

Fairy-Tale Cottage

After Jerry graduated with his bachelor's degree in theology, he got a job as an assistant pastor in a small, traditional church, making a whopping $18,000 a year. We felt like real adults.

The changes taking place at work and in our family soon led us to venture out on drive-bys to house hunt in nearby neighborhoods. To my delight, a cute cottage had just become available. It looked like a cabin in the woods with its dark-brown exterior and red-and-white checkered café curtains. But when I squinted, I could picture it all painted and bright. I knew it would be adorable.

Our first look inside did not disappoint. It was everything we had dreamed of, complete with some charming details, such as wood walls and pedestal sinks. It even smelled like freshly baked chocolate-chip cookies. Much to my husband's surprise, the condo would not be the nicest home we ever lived in. We signed the papers and got the keys to our very first "real house."

Not long after this decision, my husband got his dream job as the music pastor in a new, contemporary church. The upside was that he could often work from home and help care for our daughter Kylee. The downside was that the paycheck didn't cover our mortgage. So we got creative. Jerry took a job cleaning a health club at night, and I went back to work full-time during the day. One step forward, two steps back. That's kind of how life goes on the journey to a dream, right?

We couldn't afford to decorate, but I enjoyed puttering around that little house. We had hand-me-down wicker porch furniture in our living room. I splurged on one-size-fits-none outdoor cushions to make them more homey. We had another baby, Courtney, and both our daughters shared a tiny dormer bedroom. I loved hearing them wake up together each morning laughing and talking.

As soon as Jerry made a full-time salary, I switched back to part-time work and dove in to decorating. I bought a very grown-up, English-country-style sofa I couldn't actually afford, and I started to decorate my house around it. Other than that splurge, I was budget conscious and worked with what we had. We painted our walls linen white and the trim bright white. My mom made our curtains, and I learned how to make repairs with random fixes like stuffing corks in holes of plaster walls to make them smooth. I painted furniture and scoured garage sales for accessories. I even tried painting a wingback chair with fabric paint. Good thing I didn't have a blog back then because it was an embarrassing DIY fail. My family has referred to that wingback as the Velcro chair ever since.

When our girls started playing outside more often, we realized how busy our street was and how there were no sidewalks for taking evening family walks. Fortunately, we did have a perfectly sized, fenced back-yard, but the hope grew for a quieter street where we could go to block parties and visit with neighbors.

Even though we loved that little fairy-tale cottage, we decided that our active family would be more content a few neighborhoods over.

Picket Fences for the Win

We sold our precious cottage and moved. I was sad to close that first-house chapter of our life story, but I recall the excitement of moving on to a new (to us) house with all-new decorating opportunities waiting for me. The new house was bigger with a very charming grand living room and a picket fence. Need I say more? And the house had a quaint attic space that would make the perfect playroom. Ideas were flowing.

The large, established property was filled with good-smelling plants and flowers. Right after the move, I called my mom and told her we were living in the Garden of Eden. I could step right outside my door and cut fresh flowers!

My heart for decorating was also blossoming in this space. I pored  over magazines, ripped out my favorite ideas, and assembled them into notebooks. Each page represented a dream I had for my home. Our update to the kitchen with new counters and curtains turned out very similar to one of those magazine features, and our version was done on a meager budget.

This kitchen makeover gave us confidence and fueled more ideas. We painted the walls of our girls' tiny rooms with stripes. I learned to install a faucet and a tiled counter all by myself. We even hiked up a mountain to gather flagstone, which Jerry used to create a beautiful walkway.

Our dream house was taking shape.

Three Things I Learned from the Picket-Fence House

1. Living within your means brings more contentment than struggling to get what you don't have.

2. Visiting the neighborhood park can be as enjoyable as owning a big yard—and it's a lot less work.

3. Opening your home and heart to others will change your life. It's a risk worth taking because you'll always grow in the process.

The best part of having a home is sharing it. We eagerly opened our home to friends and family, hosted marriage groups and kids' birthday parties, and added a new member to our family —a Westie puppy named Winston.

Life was sweet in many ways, but the shine of the dream life in this house slowly started to dim. The large, lush yard that lured us in cost us every available vacation day and dollar. What good is paradise if you're too exhausted to enjoy it? The enchanting playroom I fixed up in the attic became a playground for freeloading mice. And though we loved walking to the library and shops, most of the neighborhood did not have sidewalks. And as for block parties…not a one.

During this time, we left the church we had helped start years earlier. It was a dark season filled with uncertainty. The stress of sudden social, family, and financial changes brought on a terrible case of anxiety in me. I basically turned into an agoraphobe for a few months. I lost sight of everything I loved to do and couldn't even walk out my own door without my heart racing. I felt more out of control and further from my dreams than ever before.

Out of that uncertainty emerged a next step. My husband went back to school, and we borrowed money to live. We started a house church with friends. Somehow during this time of change, it seemed like a good idea to move again. As long as we were changing everything else about our life, why not add a little more stress, right?

Apparently we are gluttons for punishment. Or maybe just dreamers.

Downsized Dreams

Slowing down to smell the roses had become a necessity for me and my emotional well-being. I was certain I was ready for less yard and more living. Downsizing sounded great!

I scoured the real-estate ads, and much to my delight, I found a small English cottage for sale in my dream neighborhood on the east side of Portland. The house and yard were  teeny tiny, which sounded just right for the manageable life I was craving.

We put dream house number two up for sale. After weeks of covering up the smell of dead mice with pungent flowers during open houses and watching six offers fall through, we finally sold our house and were able to move into the little cottage. *Now we're on the right track*, I told myself. Finally, I had found *it*—the best place for us.

The house was definitely small enough for us to keep up with, and the heavenly neighborhood had sidewalks and block parties. After waking up to the sounds of hammers and circular saws—evidence of neighbors improving their own dream cottages—I called my mom (so giddy I could barely speak without happy tears flowing) to tell her I was SO HAPPY in this house. This was where I was supposed to be, surrounded by my people—fellow house lovers.

Three Things I Learned from the Cottages

1. There is a lot of family togetherness in a small house.

2. You don't necessarily need a bigger house. You might just have too much clutter.

3. Planting your own garden is good therapy.

When we added baby number three, our son, Luke, and I started taking care of my newborn nephew during the day, the tiny house became more cramped than quaint. I was determined to make our home evolve with our family. We squished two baby swings and play-pens into our eight-by-eight dining room. We used our basement and backs of doors as pantry storage space. Still, I couldn't figure out how to organize all our clutter. My biggest fear was of our fire alarm going off in the middle of the night and firemen showing up before I had a chance to clear a path for them. Random and completely irrational worries kept me up at night. I needed an intervention.

I'm certain our house wasn't really all that bad. But I recognized that I needed order and beauty to make me happy and sane. Thank goodness I found FlyLady.net during one of my desperate days. Her advice for organizing time and cleaning schedules helped me establish order. (Ironically, they were the same lessons my mom had tried to teach me when I was growing up.)

Once I had a plan, I enjoyed mastering my newfound homemaking skills. I longed to be gracious and welcoming to guests (and firemen) and to tackle all the tasks of motherhood with a smile on my face.

Jerry and I were enjoying the stability of a calmer and cleaner home, but a different part of life became unmanageable. With two tweens and two toddlers under my charge, I spent endless hours taking my girls to and from their school, which was located on the other side of the river. Sporting events added even more round-trips. My vision of a simpler life had not included marathon minivan treks with toddlers throwing sippy cups at my head from the backseat and having diaper blowouts 45 minutes away from home.

I had swung the dream house pendulum too far east. This wasn't peaceful. At all.

Arriving at the Castle

I started to rationalize another move. If only we lived really close to the school, life would be better. It made perfect sense. So I began looking at ads. Just in case.

That's when I saw it.

Oh, my word, y'all (said in my best "maybe I should have been born in the South because everything sounds more charming" drawl). My eyes almost popped out of my head. There it was in the *Oregonian* real-estate section: THE CASTLE I HAD ALWAYS DREAMED ABOUT!

It wasn't a real castle, mind you, but the 1930s English Tudor home with 4800 square feet was as close to my childhood fairy-tale dreams as one could imagine for a couple on a normal budget. Did I mention it even had a ballroom? Now, lest you imagine something picture-perfect, let me share that it was such a wreck that it nearly left me speechless when I saw it. And by a wreck I mean there were raccoons on the roof and rats under the kitchen sink. The Realtor covered the entire kitchen island with duct tape and trash bags in a failed attempt to contain the smell of rodents. The scent was so horrible I seriously wished I didn't have a nose.

Our Realtor called it the "shock-and-awe house." It had it all—beautiful mahogany woodwork, original combed-plaster walls, wide-plank and pegged oak flooring, three grand staircases, and gorgeous antique lanterns everywhere. It also had the ugliest 1980s remodeling efforts known to man. Some decor was so bad, I almost wished I didn't have eyes.

And I'm not exaggerating, not even a little.

But it was *so* full of dreamy potential.

Now for wealthy people or DIY-ambitious buyers, this house, particularly in its sought-after neighborhood, was an investor's gold mine. However, we had come to the painful realization in recent years that (a) we were not actually wealthy, and (b) frustrating DIY projects threatened our marital unity.

A fixer-upper of this scale was obviously not the right choice if we wanted a happy, simple, manageable life. I was trying to be sensible and was 100 percent ready to walk away.

But in an ironic turn of events, my husband had evolved into a lover of beautiful dream houses just like me.

What happened to the guy who said, "This is the best house we will ever live in" back in that first condo? How did we end up as an impossibly complicated, financially strapped, dream-house-chasing, un-DIY-inclined couple who weren't content to grow old in a regular rambler?

We must have been out of our minds. So, of course, we bought it. Ridiculous.

We moved in during a snowstorm. It was so cold in that giant, uninsulated house that I lived under the bed covers for the first week, certain we had made the biggest house-buying mistake in the history of real estate. We spent the next few winters trying to reduce heat bills by wearing coats, hats, and ear muffs in the house. My dad doubled over with laughter when we greeted him at the front door wearing mittens and parkas.

As if the prospect of freezing to death in our own home wasn't traumatic enough, I also awakened one night to the horrific sound of rats clawing their way out from under the kitchen sink. That was enough to make me wish I didn't have ears. You can't unhear that sound.

This house was one huge assault on my senses. Empowered with our arsenal of creative concealers and a set of parents willing to work for free, we ripped out cigarette-smoke infused wallpaper, painted dingy plaster walls in a fresh coat of white, took out plush padded blue toilet seats, and hung curtains to minimize drafts. Among other costly repairs, we installed new furnace and electrical systems, putting a damper on dreams of prettier fixes.

So we updated the house any way we could, including hijacking everyone's birthday as an opportunity to improve the house. The highlight of my daughter's sixteenth birthday was tearing open the gift wrap to find a brand-new toilet seat. I'm pretty sure she is scarred for life.

Three Things I Learned from the Castle

1. If it smells like a dead rodent, it probably is a dead rodent. (Don't let it ruin your Thanksgiving dinner.)

2. Don't stop dreaming. Just explore new possibilities with a fresh set of eyes.

3. Trust the lessons you've learned. Repeating the same mistakes will likely bring about the same results.

We spent a year cooking quesadillas on an electric skillet in a bathroom while trying to figure out how I could design a dream kitchen on a tiny budget. Once I found a contractor willing to be creative, we started to remodel. Considering our limitations, it turned out beautifully. I started to fall in love with our home.

In many ways, living in a huge house was wonderful. We could take long, ambling walks to peek in rooms we hadn't seen in weeks. And we enjoyed having space for large neighborhood gatherings and teen hangout times. But the big old house, just like our previous big yard, demanded an exceedingly *big* investment of money and time. Sadly, the ballroom that initially captured our hearts was too expensive to heat and enjoy. Only during our Christmas parties, when we were caught up in the spirit of giving, did we crank up the thermostat. And in spite of our best efforts to make the rats feel unwelcomed for holiday gatherings, they continued to invite themselves into the walls to die just before guests arrived.

But this time, instead of picking up the real-estate ads to change our circumstances, I changed my perspective on contentment.

Not All Who Wander Are Lost

> Not that I speak from want; for I have learned to be content in whatever circumstances I am. I know how to get along with humble means, and I also know how to live in prosperity; in any and every circumstance I have learned the secret of being filled and going hungry, both of having abundance and suffering need. I can do all things through Him who strengthens me.
>
> —PHILIPPIANS 4:11-13

I spent two years soul-searching instead of house hunting, unsure of what I was looking for. I wandered back through my dream-house journey, reviewing the many ups and downs we encountered in each house. They hadn't brought the contentment I was searching for, but they also hadn't disqualified me from someday finding it.

After experiencing all those house shapes, sizes, and locations, I recognized that in every situation, we always had everything we needed to create a beautiful life at home.

I believe this is true for you too. Your house is enough. And you have enough to make it your home. Take a deep breath and soak in that little gem!

A house doesn't need to be in the perfect setting to have ambience. It doesn't have to be perfectly sized to be a great fit for your family. And a house doesn't need fancy accessories to be

Life IS FULL OF SURPRISES SO YOU MIGHT AS WELL JUST expect THEM & EVEN welcome THEM ON THE DOORSTEP YOU ALREADY HAVE

meaningful. We won't find contentment in a perfect house. We find it anywhere we learn to create a home.

That doesn't mean you and I should never move voluntarily or desire a new place. After all, not all who wander are lost—they're just gathering inspiration, right? We just need to keep perspective because jobs will come and go, belongings will break and need fixing, seasons and goals for your family change, and finances go up and down. Something will likely pull that pretty rug (or house) out from under you right after you buy the "perfect" one. Life is full of surprises, so you might as well just expect them and even welcome them on the doorstep you already have.

Whether all my moves were justified or just crazy and inefficient attempts to solve sometimes silly problems, I can't say for certain. I'm sure they have been a mix of both. But I know I am sometimes ridiculously impatient and quick to take matters into my own hands.

I have since learned to appreciate the unforeseen beauty that delicately unfolds when we let go of control and trust in the One who holds our future.

After living the house-hopping life for so long, I was tired of searching. I was ready to quit running on the squeaky hamster wheel, trying to arrive at perfect circumstances. Instead, I would start considering what contentment actually felt like and what was required to live in it.

I craved simplicity. I wanted to slow down and feel gratitude for what I already had. I wanted to stop looking for something more beautiful beyond my reach and just embrace the daily pleasures and things I learned to love in every single house.

As I reflected on all the houses that now held pieces of my heart, I was suddenly and painfully aware of how much time, money, and energy we had expended. After all those moves, we STILL didn't have it perfectly right. That was discouraging.

Part of me wished I could rewind the clock and go back for a big do-over (minus several moves). But since I couldn't go back, and since

I was still grateful for every home I had the opportunity to live in, I wanted to remember what I learned and move forward with purpose and more clarity. Now I was on a new kind of mission. Not to find another house, but to be content with the house I had.

This time I was determined that things would be different because I was different. I wanted to live more intentionally and authentically. The house would just be icing on the cake going forward. Through each and every move, I learned one thing for sure: Happiness doesn't have just one address.

You might be in a house you consider just a stepping-stone to your dream house, or maybe you're stuck in one you don't think you'll ever be happy with. But I'm confident you can find contentment while you are there and have fun making it a home! Keep dreaming.

The Inspired Room

I was finally learning the art of contentment, yet I sensed there was still something out there for me to do. But if I wasn't going to search the real-estate section for answers, where would I find them?

In a way I couldn't explain, I was restless to move in some new mysterious direction, but I was also completely content to stay put in our house. Our kids were all in school full-time, so I had more time on my hands. I wanted to use this new season to serve others in some way, but I had no special gifts to offer. I wasn't an expert at anything.

So what in the world was I supposed to do? My husband suggested helpful things I could accomplish with my restless energy, like maybe clean the closets. Nope.

I wasn't used to sitting still. But I waited and listened.

Then one day in January 2007, I woke up in that drafty castle with great clarity and the overwhelming sense that my search was over. What? I already had everything I needed.

I had a house-shaped gift.

And it was enough.

I laughed. Perhaps my house-loving self wasn't so crazy after all. All my dreams, my love of decorating, a passion for creating a meaningful home, my failures and successes in housekeeping, years of ups and downs and lessons learned and even my moves—they were all prompted by a gift that stirred my soul and made me feel more alive. Contrary to my fear, I didn't have to be an expert to have a purpose; I just had to be me. I was relieved.

On that chilly January morning I leaped out of my cozy bed, grabbed my parka, and ran to my computer to start a business out of my home called The Inspired Room. I was excited to help women create homes they loved, to help them be inspired by who they were and what they already had!

But the transformation in my life didn't stop with the newfound contentment in my home, the opportunities to help others, or the blog I started. During that year, I pried open my hands and offered my dream house back to God. *You can take it*, I said. Not because I wanted to move or find another house, but because I needed to surrender it all. *Send our family to another state, move us to an average house in a different neighborhood, or keep me here in this big house. I'm ready to quit chasing perfect circumstances, and I will willingly move or stay. I'll go wherever You send us.*

The prayer offering was a pretty big deal to me, the girl whose heart almost stopped at the thought of accepting a condo as her forever house so many years earlier. My husband hardly recognized me. I don't give up a house without finding a better one first. I was as surprised as he was that I was completely calm and content with the unknown of whatever would happen next.

It felt great to finally let go and linger in the hope of an unfolding story I didn't try to write myself.

The Craftsman House

Shortly after I released my grip on a perfect dream house and gladly eased into contentment, my husband's job unexpectedly ended. Of course it did. Because life isn't perfect, and just when you think you are content with how far you've come, more puzzle pieces scatter, and you have to figure out how to pick them all back up again.

Everything we had depended on began to shift, and the familiar ground beneath us was shaky. Month after month went by with no answers and no job offers. We knew what this meant. We could no longer support life in the castle. Moving again was inevitable.

We had been preparing our house for sale in anticipation of the worst. There were so many unfinished projects, and they all required money we didn't have. And this time, selling our home wasn't going to bring us a better house. It was simply the responsible thing to do after nearly a year without an income. It was either that or remain paralyzed and sink.

My blog was an increasingly rewarding part of my life, and it was a gift I loved to give, but it paid only in pocket change. Without the security of a family-wage job for either one of us, what would we do next? I had already surrendered our home, so I knew that moving was going to feel much different than it had before. It was scary not being able to solve the problems we faced by searching for a house, but I was strangely at peace and ready for the adventure.

I had visions of becoming a homeless home blogger.

In that season of unemployment, we found ourselves facing a snowstorm—literally and figuratively. It was a challenging time for my husband too, filled with a lot of uncertainty. Finally the fog lifted, and we saw a glimpse of where we were going.

In January 2009 we forged ahead in a frightening and exhilarating snowy move to Washington to start a church. Church planting had been my husband's ultimate dream, and in some ways this move to a new state had been my greatest fear. I was leaving the safety and familiarity of what I had always known.

Yes, a new house came with this new season in life, but I viewed our move to a rental house, a craftsman-style home on the Kitsap Peninsula, through a completely different lens than any of our other moves.

I was excited about the opportunity to test out a life of contentment and inspiration in that new home, even though (and maybe especially because) this would not be the home of our dreams. Moving to this home and starting a new life was a big risk in many ways. It took nine months to sell the castle, and we had to rent our new house, unsure whether we could ever buy it.

We lost our entire life savings because of unemployment, maintenance of two homes, and our costs during the first two years of church planting. Yet we've faced the challenges and uncertainties with hope. And—surprise, surprise, and high-fives—we are still in that craftsman home today. *Phew!* I've finally reformed my ways and stayed put through it all.

Through all the ups and downs, changes and moves, I still enjoy the journey of finding contentment right where I am. I really believe it's a lifelong process.

Even if I never again move to a house with a picket-fence, a picturesque cottage, or a sprawling castle, I love the home I have.

Once in a while I still stare a little too long at a beautiful house for sale. And I occasionally let out a flustered sigh over my imperfect house or my DIY and housekeeping fails (let's be real here), but my dream-chasing, house-loving self is more settled and content here than I ever imagined. For now, this is home.

On that cold day back at the castle, I let go of my house and offered God everything and anything I had. And do you know what? God provided our family with an exciting life purpose that aligned with His heart. And He has also been giving me the dream house I had been searching for all along.

I hope my stories and gentle encouragement in the rest of this book will inspire you in your own house adventures and even save you the hassle of striving for things you may not need. Mostly, friend, I hope and pray this book will help you to see the beauty in what you already have.

Consider This

In what ways have you been shaped by homes you've lived in?

How have life's ups and downs brought you to where you are now? *When we look at our personal history with grace and gratitude, we can better appreciate where we are in our journey.*

In what ways could you stop chasing perfection and start embracing your dreams right where you are?

Is there something you need to let go of today so you can embrace something new? *This isn't always easy but the freedom and blessing is worth it.*

CHAPTER 3

Goodbye, Unrealistic Expectations

Life's challenges are not supposed to paralyze you,
they're supposed to help you discover who you are.
BERNICE JOHNSON REAGON

I think we all long for that sacred space that invites us to relax and recharge after a day of living our crazy daily reality. We want to wake up to a home and life we love every day. Whether we are winging it or we have our bucket list all filled out, complete with five- and ten-year plans, we all have a dream about how our story is supposed to go.

When we're just starting out with a new set of house or condo keys in hand, most of us are full of youthful energy. We're optimistic for how things will be. We've got this. We too can live the dream. All we need is a Prince Charming with carpentry skills or a bit of money and a few tutorials! We start out full speed ahead on the path, eager with hopeful expectation that we will arrive at our dream house.

But if you've paid your share of rent or mortgage payments, added a kid or two, and been around the block party a few times, you might be carrying a suitcase full of decorating or homemaking mistakes and a few unfulfilled expectations. The weight of that baggage might make you wonder if you'll ever make it to where you want to be.

No matter where you are in the journey, it's wise to fasten your seat belt and get ready for the adventure. There can be lots of peaks,

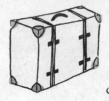 valleys, bumps, potholes, and dead ends (or dead rats) on the road to a home you love. But together we'll learn how to reframe unrealistic expectations or disappointments into hopeful expectations and find contentment wherever we call home.

Mirror, Mirror on the Wall

You've probably heard that our home should reflect who we are and what we love. That's great if we like what we see.

But what if the reflection staring back at us scares us? GASP! What if our home tells us we are a complete disaster and we need to lose a lot of (ahem) excess clutter? GULP! Who wants to hear that? I mean, each of us is a little bit of a mess, but what if the image in the mirror is a complete train wreck?

Our house is supposed to be a sanctuary, and when it doesn't reflect the peace and harmony we want, we feel as if we have failed housekeeping 101. It's embarrassing. So we turn the mirror around and blame our spouse or our kids. If they weren't so messy and would listen to us once in a while, this house wouldn't be a disaster! I know. I've done it too. I've seen friends do it. There's enough blame to go around.

Of course, a lot of us also blame ourselves and are quick on the draw to shoot down our best intentions with guilt. I remember one particular late morning, a few months after I had my second daughter, when I decided to work out instead of clean the house. It had been a while since I had tidied up, but waiting one more morning wasn't going to hurt.

Or so I thought.

As I started to sweat, I was proud of myself for doing my workout video (bonus points!) and was certain I had made the right choice. That is, until I heard the doorbell ring and caught a glimpse of my neighbor standing on our front steps. A quick look around the house proved what I already knew—my house was far from welcoming. Dishes were piled high, and laundry was everywhere. And I didn't need a mirror to tell me I was a scary sight (and smell). My hair was in an unkempt ponytail, I hadn't showered, and I had baby barf on my shoulder.

At that point, all I could do was duck under the table and hold my breath while hoping for the love of all things right in the world that my three-year-old wouldn't go running to the door. It was a harrowing couple of minutes before my neighbor walked away. As I came out from hiding, I took a deep breath and nearly inhaled a big dust bunny.

How did I become this crazy woman hiding under the table? My house was not a reflection of the home I wanted to live in, and my actions did not reflect the person I wanted to be.

Yes, in that moment I probably should have set aside my pride, opened the door, and welcomed my neighbor inside. But then I would have apologized for the state of the house, pointing out the dirty dishes and the overflowing garbage can, and then explained (um, lied) that I was wearing threadbare Snoopy pajama pants only because my stylish workout pants were in the wash.

Obviously I didn't give my neighbor a warm invitation to come in, but I regret even more that I didn't give myself grace for the life season I was in. Double fail. I was a new mom with small children. I had just fed them, and they were happy and healthy.

We can be hard on ourselves for expecting our homes to be closer to perfect and then hard on ourselves again for not being content when they aren't. When we try to find peace in unrealistic expectations of what our homes should be like, we perpetuate an endless cycle of guilt and shame.

But perhaps the tension of desiring perfection and finding contentment with what we have makes more sense than we realize. Maybe we aren't so crazy after all. We just haven't stopped to think about how we are designed.

The Story of Who We Are

My friend Emily P. Freeman wrote an inspiring book called *A Million Little Ways*. It's not a book about the home, but I was encouraged as I thought about the applications. She writes, "Maybe you are a person who thinks art is for other people. Maybe you can't imagine God having art in mind when he made you. Maybe you doubt the connection between the work you do with your hands and the story you are telling with your life."[1]

What if the state of our home matters to us because the home we create is our art, and in our heart we really do want it to tell the story of who we are? When the sound of the doorbell tempts us to duck under the table, it is because we see our mess as a reflection of our failure. We feel as exposed as Adam and Eve in the Garden of Eden when they realized they were naked and reached for the nearest, largest leaves. We understandably don't want to put that awkward moment of shame in our story (trust me on this), so we hide.

We were created in the image of God, so our desire for order makes perfect sense. I believe our longing for beauty hints at our identity as a reflection of our Creator rather than a flaw in our character.

I said it before and I'll say it again: Our desire to improve our surroundings isn't perfectionism. Perfectionism is an unhealthy trait and never leads to contentment. But setting a healthy goal and striving toward it can help us learn new skills, pick ourselves up from a slump, grow to become the people we want to be, and make positive changes in our homes. When we feel uncomfortable with where we are, that can be just the inspiration and motivation we need to look for ways to turn our struggle into progress.

When we recognize the inner soul-struggle against the mess we face and understand why we want things to be put back together again, we can crawl out from under the table. Thankfully, our stories don't end with us sprawled facedown under a pile of laundry on our living room floor. In fact, our home stories are just beginning and are full of hope. Today is a new day. We can pick up our dreams and reset the course to a home that reflects who we want to be.

Rome Wasn't Built in a Day

Patience is not one of my favorite virtues. When I get a bee in my bonnet, just like good ol' feisty Nellie Olesen on *Little House on the Prairie*, I clench my hands and stomp my feet and make it clear that I want it out *now*. When our expectations exceed our ability to keep up or make progress with what we have, we have some adjusting to do for our own sanity and for that of the people around us.

Like everything good in life, falling in love with our home takes time. We have to start with what we have, right where we are now. We can take a step in the right direction. Even if you can afford to go out and buy everything you want to make over your whole house this weekend, making selections slowly and letting your home evolve gives you the opportunity to discover what you love and feel grateful for each step.

The slow process of designing a home over time makes the journey personal and rewarding. It's in the vulnerability of imperfection that beauty really shines. No matter what you start with, each new discovery and addition is so exciting! Even if you are only rearranging what you have, you can refresh your home and love it more and more.

Being in a rush to finish can cause you to buy things that aren't necessarily the best choices in the long run. It's not about making your home perfect, but making it perfect for you! You can create a home that enhances your life right now, but at each point along the way it may look different. Take heart. Your life will evolve, and so will your home.

I spent several years thinking about our living room in our current house. It was a small, awkward space. Basically it was like a pass-through hallway from the front door to the dining room. At first I tried to set it up with the regular living-room furniture we had. It never felt right, but at least our furniture had a home while we got settled into other rooms. When we painted the walls, we liked it a little more. Then we tried different furniture arrangements. Every time my husband came home, the living room was different. If he ever went downstairs late at night, I had to warn him to pay attention to where he was walking lest he run into an end table that wasn't there a few hours earlier.

Finally I realized why it felt wrong. It wasn't working for us as a traditional living room. We didn't need another living space—we used our family room and TV room on a regular basis. We walked through the maze of furniture in the living room on our way to other rooms, but we rarely, if ever, sat down there. The room started to feel like a gathering place for chairs, not people. It overwhelmed me.

It took several years for us to recognize that what we actually needed in our home was a little more breathing room to welcome people and an overflow space where an extra dining table could be set up for large gatherings. Once we realized how we wanted to use the area formerly known as the living room, we made progress toward furnishing an intentional and functional space.

When you need to get a new view of your home...

- look at a room as though you're a visitor and observe what welcomes you and what doesn't

- spend ten minutes decluttering a space and notice the increase in peace

- consider how a room could be used in a better way for you and then try it out

- move a piece of furniture or an accessory to a new location in your house and see what creativity it inspires

We tend to love what we use the most. If you have one of those awkward areas in your home, it may never feel right until you give

Blogger *Home* ♥ *Love* Story

Don't Give Up on Your Dreams!

Years ago, when my husband and I built our colonial-style house, we didn't have enough money to add the porch we longed for. My vision of a veranda big enough for parties and cozy enough for afternoon tea motivated me to scrimp and save. When we had enough money, the technology bubble burst and sent our dot-com business south. We lived off our dream-porch fund and eventually depleted it. This cycle happened again a couple years later. During this difficult season, I learned to appreciate everything we *did have*.

After 17 years of waiting, we finally had the reserves to invest back into the house. Two decades is a long time to defer a dream, but the time was worth it—both in the lessons we learned and in the space we gained to welcome our friends and family with grateful hearts.

—Jen Schmidt, of the blog
Balancing Beauty and Bedlam

it a purpose and make memories living in the space. That process of discovering what you love and how you use your home takes time, and that's okay.

Reframe It

When we moved into our current house, we had no money to invest in projects or new things. That was a blessing in disguise because it forced me to think creatively about what I could do rather than what I couldn't buy.

My girls and I wanted to update their bathroom by adding art to the walls. On our budget of nothing, we had to get creative. We evaluated our stash of mismatched frames and decided that when we used them together, the various styles would look intentionally eclectic. The trouble was that our frames had random-sized openings, and no art would fit in them correctly.

Rather than buy new custom art, frames, or matting, we used what we had. We photocopied images from children's books, pulled together a few prints we had previously found on Etsy.com, and reframed a few pieces gathered from around our house. To fit the art into our random-sized frames, we taped each image to the cardboard inserts or onto paper cut to fit in the frames and called it done. It wasn't perfect, but it was cute enough! No one has served us with a decorating failure citation for not professionally framing our art, so no harm done.

—Style Notes—

If you've been stuck in a decorating slump for a long time, today is a perfect day to start something new. Look around and find one corner you could improve. Clean up some clutter. Or pick out a new paint color for that coffee table you've always wanted to change. It's amazing how energizing it is to stop procrastinating and get something done.

Sometimes a problem might feel like a setback, but if we reframe it (figuratively and sometimes literally!) we can see it as an opportunity. You can say, "Woe is me, I don't have enough money to get a new table, and I really don't like the oak one I have." Or you can say, "I bet if I painted this table I would love it—at least more than I do now."

The home we have right now can be perfect for us in this season. It's where we can find joy growing in our ability to manage and beautify what we have in a way that reflects who we are today. Art is a process.

And like anything beautiful and worthwhile in this world, it takes time. The challenge is to give ourselves grace and a little TLC while we and our homes are in process.

Pinterest Fails

Have you seen those funny photos posted by people who attempt fabulous Pinterest projects but end up with disasters? You'll see the Pinterest version in one photo and the mocking "Nailed it!" version in the other. If you haven't seen Pinterest Fails, you'll have to look it up for a good laugh. They make me double over giggling hysterically every time because my DIY projects are more likely to be in the fail category than the Pinterest-perfect one. I totally relate to the messy, unrecognizable glob of frosting on the cupcake that is supposed to look like Cookie Monster.

I'm a DIY-challenged blogger. (Yes, that might seem like an oxymoron, but I'm one of a kind.) My mom is way more skilled at such ventures than I am, but even she has had her funny fails over the years. She once made a small hooked rug that was intended to be a stylish, geometric shape. She hung it on the wall over our family room sofa as art. But when my sister and I looked at it, we thought it looked like a human ear.

That's just how DIY projects end up sometimes. They might look like an ear on the wall or a blob of blue frosting with unrecognizable eyeballs instead of a fluffy Cookie Monster cupcake. You never know how a project will turn out until you try. And if you don't get the desired results on the first attempt, you're not a failure. You just need to try again or find a new way to get the job done.

Every time I am contacted by a home-improvement store to partner on a project, I have to awkwardly let them know the truth. "I don't know how to use power tools, I don't like to paint, and I hyperventilate if I have to go into the lumber section alone." I actually think they hire me with the hope that if I can do something scary like use a jigsaw to cut out a monogram wood letter without cutting off my finger, I might inspire other DIY-challenged gals to try it too.

Being a DIY-challenged blogger is a big responsibility, but after I work up my nerve to try something and get a little practice, DIY projects often aren't as intimidating as they first seemed. Once I wanted a big glass lamp but couldn't afford to buy one. So on a whim, I took a big risk and bought an old glass water jug to make a lamp out of it all by myself. And I succeeded! Who knew I could make a lamp without electrocuting myself? And pretty soon that lovely DIY blue glass lamp was all over Pinterest and featured by *Better Homes and Gardens* in one of my few better-known DIY success stories.

I'm so proud of my first lamp. Now that I know how easy it is, I'm inspired to make a lamp out of everything I see. I'm not an expert, and I realize my methods would make a professional cringe or die laughing, but you can rest assured that if I can successfully do a project, so can you.

My girls and I often laugh about our miss-the-mark attempts. We really have no idea what we're doing most of the time—we just keep trying and hope that now and then something will turn out. Even when we succeed, there is usually some part that fails. We proudly made a table lamp out of a small oak barrel we found at a flea market, but in the process of drilling a hole for the cord, the drill bit fell out and dropped inside the barrel, where it remained irretrievable. Classic. You win a few, you lose a few. But if you can laugh even when you lose, it will make the whole experience way more fun for everyone in your home.

Courage to Give It a Try

Why do we think we have to have all the time, answers, and skill before we start something? And why do we give up so easily when all we really need to do is pick ourselves up and try again? Pinterest makes everything look doable because bloggers are good at breaking things down into manageable ten-step projects with neat little graphics and the big reveal "after shot." Bloggers aren't necessarily trying to convince you that it will be easy, but most of us have a lot of practice failing. I would bet that a few tears and a bit of help happen behind the scenes before a really great project makes its shiny showing on Pinterest.

I feel it is the responsible thing to do to also mention that if you are married, it takes time and communication with your spouse to figure out how to work as a team on house projects. It also takes a while to know what brings you closer and what threatens your sanity and stability as a couple. A dream house isn't worth anything if it costs you your marriage.

The upkeep of a home and family while juggling DIY and remodeling projects can take a toll on most anyone. It's so easy for communication lines to get tangled when you are in a stressful situation or under pressure. If your plans for your house are coming between you and your spouse in any way, it's time to reevaluate your expectations and priorities so your marriage can flourish. Don't let a house or your pride tear apart your home.

Come visit me on my blog, where I can point you to some easy DIY ideas that are unlikely to cause death or injury and most likely won't end with you in tears and your spouse on the couch tonight. Many of my favorite projects take about five minutes or only have a few steps because I have the attention span of a toddler.

There are many things you can do right now, with your skill and resources, to make progress on a home without losing your sanity or risking life and limb. Start with something easy and not too risky, such as hanging art on the wall or rearranging your furniture. There's always the chance you'll fail at something or shed a few tears along the way, but hopefully you can find a lot more to laugh about.

And as long as you don't get electrocuted or inadvertently tear your house down trying to meet your own unrealistic Pinterest expectations, it's all good. You can do this.

Tell Me About It

Write about a time when you had high hopes for a home project but ended up failing miserably or learning a great lesson in grace. Then come share your home love story with me at homelovestories.com, and we can laugh at our DIY fails together! *Sometimes it does us a whole lot of good to laugh about our failures, learn from them, and move on! I could fill up pages of stories about my unfortunate attempts at craftiness.*

Which dream, hope, or possibility gives you courage today?

CHAPTER 4

The Freedom of Authenticity

*To know what you prefer instead of humbly saying Amen
to what the world tells you you ought to prefer,
is to have kept your soul alive.*
ROBERT LOUIS STEVENSON

One of my most memorable life experiences was to stand in the famous Musee D'Orsay art museum in Paris years ago. The beautiful impressionist paintings by Monet and other famous artists of his day are breathtaking. I stood there with my hand over my mouth as tears filled my eyes. My emotional reaction to the art surprised me, but it was quite the powerful experience to be so close to the brushstrokes of these masters.

A painting can look flat in a book or on a computer screen, but the actual art is textured and dimensional. I totally would have reached out to touch the paint had the guards not been watching me carefully. Each painting was like the unique artist responsible for it—imperfectly beautiful up close and perfectly stunning when you stepped back. I imagined how the artists chose their subjects and labored over their creations one stroke of their brush at a time, perfecting each color and layering each texture to form what would become a masterpiece.

This encounter with art inspired how I view my role as the creator of my home.

When we form a home from a place of authenticity, our uniqueness will shine through it like our own little work of art. Just like an artist, we are free to create from the heart. We can share what we've experienced and where we've been. We can reflect what we want our home to feel like when we are close up and safe inside and what we hope the bigger picture will look like as we step back and see how our efforts inspire our lives and the lives of others.

Your home is full of opportunities to express your true self. Even if you and I like the same colors or styles, your home, grand or humble, is completely yours to transform. After all, it is you, with your tastes and preferences, who has the joy of choosing...

- the way you keep house
- the mood you want to express
- how to organize your belongings
- the depth and brightness of colors
- the amount of money you spend
- what your accessories represent
- which textures and patterns define your vision
- what inspires you and what doesn't

Does creating an authentic home now seem like a daunting task when before you thought all you had to do was decide which picture to hang or what color of slipcover matches your walls? Not to worry. I love sharing tips and ideas to help you make your house more beautiful along the way. Be encouraged!

Your home is a significant part of who you are. It's also a safety net and springboard for you and your family to accomplish the many dreams you will have in your lifetime. That's why it is essential to create a home that is a true reflection of your life as a whole. It will inspire your family more than you might realize. Freedom and beauty open up when we begin with a perspective of authenticity rather than of worry, bound by rules and what-ifs. This is an adventure we don't want to rush.

What Makes You Come Alive?

Creating a home is an adventure of discovering what makes us come alive. The things that are most authentic are often the most meaningful to us. Pinterest may tempt us to click on all the beautifully finished "before and after" room makeovers, but on any given day, our own homes linger somewhere in the middle of progress.

An authentic home embraces the tension between the state of daily chaos (a.k.a living a full and meaningful life!) and the beauty of an evolving style. There is no shortcut to designing a meaningful place for your family. It's a lifelong process of creating memories and refining your style to reflect what stirs your emotions and fuels your passion for life along the way.

I love to add meaning through simple things we collect over the years that hold our memories, such as family photos, books we love, art, collections, mementos, and furnishings acquired over time. But I also create a meaningful home by setting up comfortable and inspiring places for my family to live life. We bring beauty to our experience one layer at a time. We have organizational systems to improve the way our family functions at home. We add textures and colors to make us feel alive and engaged. And even the play of light and scents makes the experience more personal and influential.

I believe we feel the most alive in our home when we sense the intangible beauty and blessing all around us. These move us to live a

-Style Notes-

Express your authentic style by surrounding yourself with layers of special memories to tell your unique story. Rather than filling your home with random accessories or things bought simply to fill a space, collect things you love in the process of living a full and meaningful life.

more grateful life. You may or may not see those things in a photo of a house, but a meaningful home isn't designed for Pinterest. Experiencing beauty is an emotional experience that doesn't always translate to what the world can see. It's all about how your home makes *you* feel.

Wear Your Rose-Colored Glasses

One of the things I crave most of all in my home is a cozy, comfortable, and inviting atmosphere for my family. At this point in our lives, my family is living a busy and very active lifestyle overseeing our church ministry, creating my books, running a business, and keeping up with each other. In many ways, we are living our dreams, and we love it.

Yet even a life we love comes with responsibilities, stress, and hard work. No matter what kind of life we live or what burdens we carry, we all crave a refuge from the outside world where we can inhale deeply, exhale slowly, and let the cares and expectations fall away. Our home is that safe place.

I love to prepare comfy corners that invite me to curl up on a rainy day with a good book. I take pleasure in shaping places to relax and cuddle up by a warm fire. I can't wait to set pretty tables where my family can dine or play games by flickering candlelight. Those are the kind of experiences I imagine as I make decisions about what I want for my home and family.

Now, I realize that romantic picture sounds dreamy but probably a bit detached from everyday life, as if I were wearing rose-colored glasses. It's probably true. We don't play games by candlelight nearly enough, right?

Yet my intention for such experiences and for those refuge spaces makes a big impression on me and a considerable impact on my choices, and I'll bet that's the same for you. Setting the right atmosphere inspires us with what is possible. Setting our minds on what is lovely around us and what *can* be lovely nurtures our hope and dreams for our home and life while also guiding how we make changes and improvements.

Do you ever stop to consider what you want your home to feel like? I don't mean which magazine or style you want it to look like, but the way you want it to feel to you when you walk through your front door. Go back to the dream house you envisioned at the end of chapter 1. Look at your list of dream features and your answers about what your dream house might be like.

How would a house like that make you feel if you were to come home to it every night? Would sweet tea on your beautiful front porch change the way you viewed your life? Would a roaring fire in your fireplace make you snuggle up to your spouse a little bit closer, a little more often?

There are no right or wrong answers to questions like these, but they can help you start envisioning and sensing what you really want from your home. It may seem silly to dream, but dreaming out loud

Creating a home ON PURPOSE frees us TO DO THE THINGS WE REALLY want to do

sometimes brings clarity and motivation and ideas you may not have considered before.

We want to create homes that are meaningful on an emotional level and fulfill our families' need for a retreat from the world. This is where we can fill up again to go back out and serve and live out our dreams outside our own four walls. Creating a home on purpose frees us to do the things we really want to do.

Putting on rose-colored glasses to see and create your home through your most romantic lens is much more inspiring than putting on the scratched, smeared ones you dug out from the depths of your purse. Allow your home to reflect your best vision of life by looking at it with authenticity, intention, possibility, and purpose.

The Greatest Escape

Do you crave relaxing vacations, like a weekend at a bed-and-breakfast? Do you dream of romantic dinners at a restaurant with the love of your life? I do! People don't laugh at us when we share those dreams aloud. They might be a bit envious, but they don't roll their eyes when we share our dream vacation plans. We can all relate to wanting such experiences of renewal and joy, and we think it's quite normal and positive for people to dream of such possible happenings.

But it's sad to realize that most people dream more about their once-a-year vacation plans than about their intentions for their home, where they live all year long! This is a great loss and may explain why many of us forget about the impact of our homes.

Maybe the dream of a pretty, relaxing, and comfortable home seems unrealistic. I mean, we do have laundry and an unending supply of dust! The image of dirty socks on the floor is not romantic. And those piles of food-encrusted dishes! You can't escape them. There are kids underfoot, turning the sofa into a fort! And let's not forget we have bills to pay. We need to get away from it all, so we dream of escaping to somewhere else. So much reality and so little time!

So you and I need to figure out something important. How can we turn our dreams back toward our homes? What will help make our homes as special as a vacation escape?

From the day Jerry and I walked into our first little cottage, and on through our many moves, we have found great joy in creating homes that were shelters for reality and also our sweet escapes. They weren't brochure-perfect, but each home had the romantic quality of being our private little getaway.

There is no place we'd rather be than home. Investing in whatever place we spend our days is always worthwhile. The house we have now provides a great example for how a place can be transformed. It lacks the old-world charm our family loves so much, but I've been determined to create spaces that offer getaway moments and inspire meaningful experiences.

In our gathering room, we have a double wingback settee sofa that invites us to snuggle up with a good book. Our gas fireplace in our family room might not be as romantic as the wood-burning ones in our old houses, but with the flip of a switch on a cold winter's day, we are warm and all aglow! Lighting candles in our home invites us to slow down, to keep the world from spinning around us, and to savor that moment. The little corners we purposefully create inspire me to love my home.

Appropriate Next Steps

One day my daughter Courtney brought a friend over to meet our one-year-old goldendoodle puppy, Jack. Her friend noticed Jack's character trait that stands out to anyone who meets him or follows him on his Facebook fan page. Between fits of giggling at his ridiculous antics, she said, "He is so inappropriate!" We laughed because she was absolutely right. He has always struggled to follow the wiser, more appropriate choice. This makes him charming and gives his fans a great chuckle, but as a result, he is a real handful.

Most of us don't tear apart rolls of toilet paper like Jack does when he gets bored or anxious, but we do make less-than-ideal decisions at times. When we are faced with exciting possibilities for our home, we don't always think through the appropriate steps or consider all the ramifications of our choices. There's plenty of room for us to dream *and* to create our own happiness right where we are as long as we balance dreams with appropriate decisions along the way (before we find ourselves like Jack, looking sheepish with toilet paper straggling behind us).

These six simple steps can help you prioritize your to-do list and find balance.

1. Think of the top two things that *need* to be done in your home.

2. Choose two things you *want* to do to your home or to a room.

3. Examine the expense of both time and money for these four options.

4. Write out a near-future plan of action to get the necessities taken care of.

5. Write out a short- and long-term plan of action to get the extras.

6. Look for temporary solutions! (For example, if you can't get new windows, hang curtains that change the look of the windows for now.)

When Jerry and I moved into our new house, it felt less like home on day one than any of our other houses. We didn't choose this house for how it felt—we chose it because it was the appropriate choice for our life at that time. We thought through our level of tolerance, our lack of time and finances for projects, our family's need for space and comfort, and the location we needed to be in to start the church my husband came to plant. An old house in this area would have consumed too much of everything.

The new house wasn't the romantic choice our other homes had been. Our previous choices were based on factors like a long-desired neighborhood, charming plaster details, and wood floors. Instead, this was a practical decision. It was more ready-made than we were used to, though even this practical choice came with some features we knew we would have to deal with—especially the wall color!

I've never liked the phrase "it's only paint." That's what you say when you like to paint and have time and money on your hands. But the pigskin-colored paint in this 2500-square-foot house has almost been the death of us. Every bit of the drywall squealed at me, mocking me from day one. My blog readers remember this color well. How could we forget the years of wiping out the swine? (I apologize to all pig lovers who might take offense to the nickname of my paint. I assure you that no pigs were harmed in the process of any project.) If you haven't read the blog yet, you'll get a good chuckle out of the old posts on those unfortunate swine-colored walls.

Do we miss the charming old houses from our past? Absolutely. Are we more content here in many ways since we made this choice? Yes. Although we feel homesick for Portland and the types of houses we've had, our earlier commitment to take the appropriate next step continues to nurture the life we want to lead in this season.

Making sacrifices to live our life as a whole, to invite in parts of ourselves that were missing in the past, gives us new perspective. As we get to know ourselves and our needs, habits, strengths, and weaknesses, we can learn to be more mindful about how we use our finances and our energy. We don't always get everything right. But along the way to our dreams, we have opportunities to make appropriate decisions to keep us on course.

We are more content in this house in many ways, so letting go of the old-house dream (for now!) has been worth the sacrifice. There were obvious things we wished were different about the house (like the swine hue), yet the patience and experience we had gleaned over the years in the older homes helped us turn this space into a home that works for our family. Perhaps a day will come when we are ready to merge our old-house love with our new-house practicality, but for now we are finding contentment here.

To make appropriate decisions, we often have to sacrifice one thing for another, but at least we have guidelines to help us make the best decisions for this time and place. When my children were young, we set up our home to accommodate their needs. We turned our master bedroom into a room for our daughters and a dining room into a playroom for our son. We lived with a secondhand, slipcovered sofa because the cover could easily be washed, so I wasn't too stressed out when our kids sat on it while eating pepperoni pizza.

It is freeing to live within your means, to have boundaries around your time, and to focus on the bigger picture of your life as you make daily decisions for the home. Considering the appropriateness of a decision for the time and season you are in helps you view the creation of your home as a lifelong process rather than a rushed event. It evolves with your family.

By the way, this is true even if your current dwelling is a short-term housing option. You are still shaping your ongoing, forever sense of home. So don't be in a hurry. There is no rush. There's no finish line. Go at a pace that makes sense for you because when you say no to a decision that isn't right for your home, you have the freedom and confidence to say yes to something better when the time comes.

Your Home's Love Language

More than any other place in the world, your home is where you should be free to be yourself. Many aspects of who you are and what you love can be incorporated into *how* you love and care for your home. Your choices can reflect love and care for yourself and for those you hold dear.

Your home can be as beautiful, colorful, tidy, cluttered, neutral, big, small, perfectly imperfect, and wonderful as you want it to be—within the realm of reason, of course. Let's not get crazy here. The point is this: It's okay to strive to create the best environment you can, given what you have to work with. That's a good way to strive—give your best and make peace with the rest.

Relationship counselor Gary Chapman's bestselling book *The Five Love Languages* encourages readers to discover how they and their loved ones best receive love—through gifts, quality time, words of affirmation, acts of service, or physical touch.[2] We all have our own love language, and the better we understand our own and that of the people in

YOU GIVE A *Gift to others* BY MAKING THEM FEEL *comfortable & welcomed* NOT BY CHANGING *who you are*

our lives, the better able we are to receive and give love. I believe we also communicate love with and through our homes. We and our family members and guests can feel loved through actions as well as special touches, ambience, and authenticity in our home.

Through all the choices you make, you are the one who will decide what your home communicates. Your home's love language won't necessarily be the same as mine. You get to make decisions about what is comfortable, what is right to your own eye, and what fits with the type of life you lead. This is your home, your sacred space. It should be a beautiful reflection of you and the other people who live there.

Your home is your own blank canvas just waiting for your special touch of art and your vision of beauty and hospitality. Others may not understand your home's love language, and some might even try to tell you how to express yourself differently. If others imply that you've done it wrong or that you are doing too much or not enough for their tastes, they are misunderstanding the purpose of a home.

When you invite a guest into your home, they are in your sanctuary. They are invited in to be themselves. You give a gift to others by making them feel comfortable and welcomed, not by changing who you are.

The more comfortable you become with nurturing your environment and who you are, the easier it will become to stop worrying about or apologizing for what you have or haven't done to clean or design your home.

You don't owe guests an apology for being you. If you are someone who loves to clean and decorate for guests and you spend a lot of time getting each detail just right, this may be how you express love. Of course, offer yourself grace to stop preparing when you feel you've done enough, but also grant yourself the wide-open freedom and joy to press on in your preparations.

It's your house, your party. You can clean if you want to!

Great Freedom

Eleanor Roosevelt said, "With freedom comes responsibility." We have great freedom in our home to create what we want. We have the freedom to be ourselves. But we also have the responsibility to ourselves and to our family to make sure it reflects the best of who we are and want to become.

If we focus only on the freedom without the responsibility, there's a chance our bad side will rule the roost. Honestly, the side of me that pulls myself together with a smile and walks out the door wearing lipstick and cute heels and who gives a cheerful wave to people I hardly know is often *way* more pleasant than the side of me that lets it all hang out at home. You know what I mean?

Our refuge is the one safe place where people are most likely to love and understand us even on our bad days. But if we are in the habit of filling our home with negativity, complaining, disrespect, selfishness, and laziness, the beauty we are trying to create will take a hit. Giving the best of ourselves to those we love at home changes the playing field. We change the atmosphere of our house by changing the tone of our words and setting the example for our home's love language.

Five Tips for an Authentic Home

1. Incorporate conversation pieces into your decor that allow visiting friends to get to know you. Sharing your family history, including the places you've been, your life experiences, and your dreams, nurtures an authentic home.

2. Limitations can spark your creative spirit! Authentic style comes from creative problem solving and addressing needs in your own unique way. What trouble area can become a place of possibility?

3. Embracing authenticity is about designing your life. Each new experience and life season offers you the opportunity to add beauty to your home.

4. Learn the art of subtlety. Incorporate significant memories into your decor without making *everything* a "Ta Da!" moment.

5. Let your home evolve. An authentic home requires time and real life to create. Don't apologize for being in process—the best rooms take time.

We have several personal pieces of art in our home that gently remind us of our love language and help us stay fluent in it. In our master bedroom, we have a lovely painted wood sign with a meaningful verse for our marriage. In our TV room, we have a framed chalkboard art print with positive reminders of healthy attitudes we want to display out of love for each other.

You Are in Style

We are surrounded by voices telling us what's in, what's out, what's hip, what's not, and whether the state of our home makes us worthy to be a friend or fit to be a parent. No wonder we all feel the need to explain ourselves over and over. How frustrating, especially when we are just trying to do our best, right?

When people judge or misunderstand you, they probably don't understand what it means to create an authentic life and home. It's risky to be who you are and share your heart and home, but authenticity is so worth it! Trust me, I know how it feels to be vulnerable, to share who I am. I put my house and heart online every day for a half a million people to see. Talk about scary! And now I'm opening up to you in this personal, one-on-one journey. But it is so worth it.

Being authentic is always in style. Put the judgment and doubt behind you. When you're more comfortable with yourself and who you are becoming, you can open your house to others and invite them to make themselves at home, slow down, connect, rest, and laugh. By opening the door, you share a vulnerable side of yourself and encourage others to do the same. Your hospitality could remind others that their authenticity is in style too.

That is what authenticity is about—being vulnerable and real with people who are in process just like you.

As you look at your own space, think of it like a blank canvas where you can pour out your heart and creativity with every brushstroke. There is no right or wrong way to express your authentic style! One layer at a time, enjoy the process of refining your home to reflect who you are and what makes you come alive. Consider all the creative details and special touches that will nurture your family and invite others in. The emotional connection we have to our home will inspire us to transform that blank canvas into a unique and authentic masterpiece.

Write It Down

What is your love language at home? *What actions, words, or behaviors help you feel loved by your family? What actions, styles, and priorities in your home help you show love to others?*

Think about how you would like your family and guests to describe the canvas of your home. *Would you want it to be a happy home, a peaceful home, an energizing home, or perhaps a warm home?*

What are some new ways you could express your authentic personality through your home?

CHAPTER 5

A Beautiful Mess

Every day God invites us to go on the same kind of
adventure. It's not a trip where He sends us a rigid itinerary,
He simply invites us. God asks what it is He's made us to
love, what it is that captures our attention, what feeds that
deep indescribable need of our souls to experience the richness
of the world He made. And then, leaning over us,
He whispers, "Let's go do that together."
BOB GOFF

Creating a beautiful home is not about presenting a perfect image to the world. It is about creating a perfect space in which to live your unique life. A well-loved home will always be a bit of a beautiful mess.

If we were to drop in to each other's home unannounced and take a peek, I think we'd find similarities. Both of us likely have some sort of mess in plain sight as well as some evidence of our desire to create something beautiful for our families.

The tolerance for messiness and the commitment to beauty in any home will be unique to each woman and each family. The key is to find the right balance. Living life intentionally helps us define and recognize the right combination of the two so our home feels more beautiful and manageable to ourselves and others.

The Well-Lived Life

Sometimes after I share on my blog a photo of a pretty, clean room from my home, a reader will post a comment about the scenario being

A Well-Loved HOME WILL ALWAYS BE A BIT OF A beautiful mess

unrealistic because they don't see dirty dishes or socks lying around. Never mind that they just scrolled past the photos with dog fur and spit flying as our pups made a game of tossing my couch cushions all over the floor.

Real life seems to get labeled as messy while anything romantic, such as a table set with the good dishes (especially if you have kids), or anything clean, such as a tidy family room, gets the bum rap as being out of reach and out of touch for everyday living.

Bah. Humbug. I disagree. But don't throw tomatoes at me. Let me explain how I feel about that around our house.

Do we have smelly socks in our home? Every single day. Do we have dirty dishes in the sink and dog-nose smudges on our windows and other signs of chaos in our home? Yes we do! I am grateful for what each of those represent, and there is beauty in that. They are evidence of a life we dearly love.

But are unsightly and smelly things the only standards by which we can measure what is true about who we are? Please, no. I don't limit the extent of my creative experience and appreciation for my home to my clever techniques for piling the dirty dishes on the counter as high as I can without them crashing to the floor.

We enjoy creating a welcoming atmosphere in our home. We also take comfort in the goodness of the undone and unraveled. Both of these are signs of contentment. Both provide evidence of lives well lived and people well loved within those four walls.

I feel the most content when I connect all the dots of what is true about the life I want to live and the home I am inspired to create. If I follow those connections, they flow from room to room through the furniture we arrange for comfort, the color we choose for ambience, and the kitchen we clean for contentment. They weave through memories of laughter and piles of laundry and remind me of the family I adore.

When we embrace all sides of our family life, we stand in the intersection of the beautiful and the chaotic. We live in the authentic here and now. This is how any house can become a home we dearly love.

Compromise offers us grace. Your home should reflect the level of comfort and inspiration you find in design styles, chaos, order, quiet, and activity. Learn to find contentment right where you are—even when your house doesn't reflect your perfect dream. The combination of loveliness and mess you create with what you have right now, as a reflection of who you are and what you love, will be evidence of a well-lived life.

The beautiful mess we create and embrace at home is a collage of everything that makes us come alive and find joy. I remind myself to smile every day when I clean our dogs' nose prints off the windows because the mischief and mayhem caused by fluffy pups are part of what makes this house our refuge. They are wanted and invited into our life, slobbery noses and all. (Actually, I don't want the slobber, which is why I take a few moments to clean up the window, but their noses stay as a part of the deal.)

Blogger *Home* ♥ *Love* Story

Releasing Control to Embrace a Home I Love

I'm an introvert and a self-professed control freak. I've always loved decorating my home, but I rarely let anyone in to enjoy it. But then I said yes to a God-sized dream that required me to let people in to my life and my home.

We sold our house in a planned community and moved to a rural area, where we also placed the USA office for Mercy House, the nonprofit our family started. This has turned our closed front door into a revolving one. Most days, we have a dozen volunteers serving. And do you know what? I love it. I haven't lost control—I've just relinquished to God my need to control. He has used my shaky yes to change my life and the lives of others and to turn my home into a hub for His glory. Saying yes in your mess is a beautiful adventure!

—*Kristen Welch, of the blog*
We are THAT Family

Our home inspires us to live well at home and to spread our wings and invest ourselves in the community around us. When our home is in order, we are more fully equipped and prepared to go out into the world and make it a better place too.

Magazine Cover-itis

I've had a lifelong love for home-decorating magazines. Even now that we can find so many beautiful images online, nothing compares to holding those glossy pages in my hand and poring over each article and photo. This has sparked a fun hobby and an education in what beautiful design looks like. It has also shaped what I'm able to envision and create for my home.

Loving anything material is risky business. Sometimes my desire for a magazine-cover-worthy home nearly cost me things I held dear. I spent too much time or money pursuing what would be pleasing to my eye rather than what would be appropriate for my family. I perceived the mess around me as unwelcome and unworthy. I became frustrated when I couldn't keep up with the perfect image for every aspect of life.

When our desire for beauty and perfection overshadows our ability to embrace an imperfect life in the here and now, we're likely to contract a disease I call magazine cover-itis. The only antidote is to embrace the balance of beauty and mess as two elements in the same, wonderful picture of authenticity.

After years of studying artfully arranged rooms on glossy pages, I never imagined that my home could be featured in one of those beloved magazines. Then one day *Better Homes and Gardens* arranged to do a photo shoot of our freshly remodeled kitchen. I was nervous, excited, and certain that I'd learn a few things. Sure enough, the photographer shared interesting perspectives on what makes a beautiful photo for readers. I came away from that experience with a new appreciation for the way we can create beauty in our homes in the midst of day-to-day chaos!

The photographer set up each scene in an appealing composition. The first thing that fascinated me was that he didn't set up the entire room to be photo-ready all at once. I had always assumed that magazines only featured homes that were picture-ready from every point of view and every angle all at the same time. This doesn't mean the

—Style Notes—

Many of our messes reflect the presence of joyful activity, loved ones, and a full life being lived. Embrace them as natural, important parts of your journey toward a home of value and purpose. You might even notice that your messes have the imprint of your own special style!

unstaged areas of a featured home are not lovely. They just aren't all magazine-ready at the same time.

Surprisingly, the magazine wasn't interested in featuring a perfectly designed vignette. Rather, the photographer composed an inspiring reflection of real life. Each image he captured represented a genuine way in which our kitchen serves our family.

After the photographer asked questions about how we used our kitchen, he pursued images that would be meaningful to readers on a deeper level than a mere pretty picture could be. He created a genuine reflection of the experiences we have enjoying our coffee station, making salad with our daughters at our kitchen island, and preparing our baking counter for a round of cookie making. By featuring our everyday accessories and activities, he told the story of life in our kitchen.

Behind the camera there was some disarray because this is where the creative process takes place. Yet the messiness we could see didn't take away from the beauty revealed in the photos. Both scenes represented our family and the story of our life at home. The pictures weren't illusions crafted for the world—they were true reflections of what we had created and what we enjoyed in our home.

The Secret to Balancing It All

When I first became the keeper of my own home and tried to navigate my way through all I needed to do, I had a lot to learn. I made many attempts to create something wonderful with our mess (and often failed). My mom had taught me what I needed to know, yet I was just discovering how to put those lessons into practice and adapt my expectations to suit what worked best for my husband and eventually our kids.

We all have to pave our own way with the gifts, circumstances, challenges, and opportunities we face. Wise women build their homes in their own unique way. Some women choose to stay home to keep up with the needs of their houses and families. Others have additional careers, working from home or in another workplace.

I've spent most of my home-building years working from home or elsewhere to contribute to my family, so I understand the obstacles and pressures most women face to balance the demands of family life and their own dreams.

Those who are married have the added challenge of incorporating another person's views and expectations about how the home will look and who will do the work in a way that pleases both parties. When you live under the same roof with someone, undoubtedly there is a period

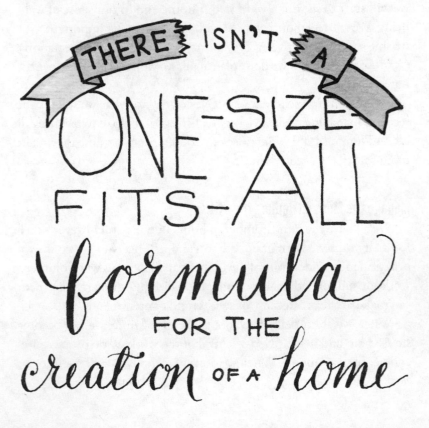

THERE ISN'T A ONE-SIZE-FITS-ALL formula FOR THE creation OF A home

of adjustment as you both function in and contribute to the home. You may not see eye to eye on what is important, and each of you is likely to cause frustration for the other.

There isn't a one-size-fits-all formula for the creation of a home. Thankfully there are many clever, flexible ways to do it well. Shaping a home with a family is an added blessing with its own challenges. There is no substitute for a mother present and active in the life of a child, but there are many options for how a mom spends her time to build a safe, nurturing home in which her family can thrive.

None of us can do it all, and we certainly can't do everything well all the time. Stay-at-home moms, working moms, and every mom in between knows how hard it is to juggle it all. We fail and flail and cry over spilled milk. We love our kids and want to do our best. So how can we do what needs to be done and do it well in spite of the challenges?

If we clarify our purpose, set goals, and use our time accordingly, we will start to see the reward in our home and in our sense of well-being. We will feel more balanced with our choices. It's important to be flexible so we don't drive everyone crazy with unrealistic expectations. On the other hand, if we don't plan at all, we won't be likely to love the home we have.

Having a purpose and a plan gives clarity to what we do. It's the secret to managing what we have. Realistic goals help us to balance our life and home, and they increase our contentment because they make room for what we truly value.

Manage the Mess to Reduce the Stress

We all have the same number of hours in our day. However, you'll feel as if you have been granted bonus hours once you get your own beautiful mess under control! Over the years, a lot of us who volunteer, work, or support others have come to realize that time management can make or break our sense of success and contentment.

When we aren't deliberate about our use of time, we can become stressed out and maybe even resentful of the work we do or the causes and people we support. When we don't accomplish all we want to, it's easy to blame our lack of time or our particular circumstances. But often the reason is a mix of factors. That's why I find it to be more productive to focus on how we manage what we have rather than create a list of excuses.

I've always been pretty busy. When I was a young woman working full-time with no kids, I struggled to keep my house clean and in good order. When I had young children and worked part-time, I still struggled to keep my house clean and organized. And when I had the opportunity to be home full-time with my kids, even then I struggled because of my growing expectations of what I could or should do in a day.

As much as I thought the problem was my lack of time, the number of kids in my care, my particular job, or whatever other excuse came to mind, I realize now that the real issue was the way I managed my time.

Now that I spend more than full-time hours to run a business, manage multiple projects and people, work with business partners and colleagues, and help with our church and family, I finally have a better handle on how to keep the house in order. It's a bit surprising! Everything is not always in its place (I am so *not* superwoman), but I find that bringing order and beauty to our life is finally a manageable goal. It's even enjoyable!

I probably have less free time than ever, but I still designate some time and space for myself. This keeps me from being overly stressed (well, at least in this moment) and allows me to deliberately create balance and room in my life for what matters.

Do I keep up better because my kids are now older or because I'm a better manager of my life and home? The answer is probably both and then some. But in this season, I have discovered more secrets than ever before to managing life and the beautiful mess that is our home.

Planning for a Beautiful Mess

I learned principles for managing the mess the hard way—through trial and error. And I am grateful because now I love to share these principles with my daughters (and anyone else wanting to listen) and to remind them that no matter what a situation looks like or what their own homes and families need someday, they can be mindful of where their time and energy goes. And then they can make choices. That's the truth for you and me too. In any season, thriving with a beautiful mess at home is much easier when we know our purpose and have a plan.

Find Purpose

Success isn't something that just happens. Usually it comes to people who have set out in the direction of their purpose. Guess what? If you don't know what your purpose is for your home, you'll never be certain how to achieve it. You won't be sure how to spend your time. Hours or even days might go by with nothing to show for them. You'll waste precious time on tangents or distractions that don't matter to you.

Thinking about your home's purpose is time well spent. And once you write it down, it will be that much easier to pursue. A purpose statement for your home doesn't have to be complicated or formal. It can be a guiding verse, a list of priorities, or a statement that defines what you would consider success in your home. Our purpose statement for our home is simple:

> *Our home is a place that honors God and serves as a*
> *restful retreat from the outside world to prepare us to*
> *go back out to love and serve others well.*

When we remember our intention for our home, we are inspired to make it everything we want it to be. And we don't feel guilty about what we don't do or can't do. It's very freeing.

Devise a Plan

Once you've defined your home's purpose, I suggest you create a few goals for this year. Your home goals should support your purpose statement and not be in conflict with it. But they are different from your purpose statement because they are the bite-sized, measurable action steps that will help you create the environment you want and achieve your purpose.

Every January, I write up a simple list of our
home goals. My free-spirited side resists writing
anything down for fear of being restricted, but
I've found tremendous value and freedom in
putting goals on paper. Once I start writing them
down, I almost consider them more like dreams
than actual goals. But either way, make a list.

One year I dreamed really big. In fact, I felt a little silly writing
down my list and sharing it on the blog because so many of my dreams
seemed far-fetched and not likely to happen in that year. But you know
what? Writing out my dreams paid off. I accomplished every single
dream on my list and more. Something about seeing dreams in black
and white was empowering and motivating.

It's been said that goals are dreams with a deadline, and I can't argue
with that. Goals point you toward your purpose and help you visualize
what it will take to achieve it. When you see your goals in writing,
you'll be inspired to focus your attention on what matters to you, and
you'll be willing to let go of what isn't as important.

Delete

One of the best secrets to success at home is to remove things from
your schedule that clutter your time and drain your energy. You simply
cannot do it all. Look at your home purpose statement and goals. Now
think about how you spend your time when you are at home. If your
first thought is, *I'm not sure where the time is going*, then keep a time log
for a day or two, writing down everything you do when you're home.
You'll probably discover that you have more time than you thought,
but much of it is going to things that aren't on your priority list.

Now that you've identified things you want to do (through your
purpose statement and your goals) and you know what you are doing
at home, think about all the other things you do or feel obligated to do
that don't support your goals. It's okay to delete even good things from
your life in this season, but don't delete activities that will help you to
achieve your goals and live out your purpose.

For instance, if you want your home to be a retreat from the world,
don't feel obligated to host weekly events at your home that might

cause undue stress. (Of course, if you love entertaining and are a bit of an extrovert, maybe hosting once a week is not enough!) If your goal is to create a gathering place, you might want to delete things in your schedule that will keep you so busy running around town that you don't have the energy to invite others to your home.

Simply restructuring your week can help you to accomplish more. For example, perhaps you want to volunteer at your church or school, or you want to spend time on causes or hobbies that are important to you. If your home seems to require too much time, set aside one day or morning a week for activities outside your house.

Such a change to your schedule will require you to fit your house-keeping and home-maintenance projects into the other days or evenings of the week. At first it seems counterintuitive to take away time to add in something new, but restructuring your time helps you to be more efficient with the remaining hours of the week.

Make a list of what *not* to do and keep it with your purpose statement and your list of goals.

Delegate

None of us can do everything all the time, so delegating is another great tool to aid your progress. If you want to do things that don't fit into your schedule no matter how disciplined you are, find a way to delegate to free up some time! The best way to do this is to focus on tasks only you can do, and if possible, delegate the rest.

Get help from your spouse and kids. Trade help with neighbors or friends, or hire some outside help so you will have more time for what you truly want to do while keeping up with what needs to get done.

Our church hosts a monthly serve day. We love helping others do projects around their houses. Our team works together to get things done for someone else in a few short hours rather than the weeks it might take for them to do it alone. Besides, it's always more fun to work with friends! You could try something like this in your neighborhood, church, or community!

Making a plan and moving forward in it alleviates the pressure that builds when the things you want to do or should do never get done.

You'll know what to expect, and you'll start to feel like a balanced person. You might have to get creative with how things get done at your house, but the effort to create a plan for balancing the beautiful mess in your home will be worth it.

Update your list of what not to do by adding other items you could delegate.

Adjust the Mix

You will need to make a series of adjustments to get the most effective mix for you, but the more you focus on clarifying your purpose, defining your goals, and deleting or delegating what you can, the easier it will get. You can add a little more beauty to the mess until you get it right for this season, or you can mix in a little more mess to allow for more beauty to shine through.

There is no way to create a perfect home. We all juggle the beautiful mess of daily life in different ways and with varying degrees of success. Be gentle with yourself as you find what works for you! Discovering your purpose and defining your goals—reviewing them and refining them over time—helps you live more fully and happily in the home you have.

Remember to see the messy evidence of a life well lived as a beautiful reminder of what you love!

Let's Take a Walk

Take a quick walk around your house and make note of three beautiful messes that are evidence of the life you live and the people you love in your home. *In my house right now are random remnants of paper that my crazy dog Jack decided to rip up and the pots and pans still on the stove from when my husband made dinner.*

What beautiful messes have you discovered today?

Now that you have toured your home, what purpose for this space comes to mind? *How do you want its best features and unique flaws to serve you, your family, and others?*

As you consider finding a good mix of mess and beauty in your life, what can you delete or delegate? *Think about a way to find more balance so you can experience the momentum and freedom of a realistic plan.*

Put your home purpose statement and goals in black and white. Your unique style, gifts, and personality will influence your purpose for your home. And your purpose statement will, in turn, continue to influence your journey toward an authentic lifestyle. *It's an incredible adventure of growth and joy...so get out your pen. To give you a place to start writing, you will find a downloadable home goal sheet at lovethehomeyouhave.com.*

CHAPTER 6

Decluttering the Nooks and Crannies

*One of the advantages of being disorderly is that one is
constantly making exciting discoveries.*
A.A. MILNE

Close your eyes and imagine what you want in your dream house. You're not likely to see rooms full of clutter, overflowing drawers, and boxes brimming with unknown stuff. Am I right? Now, open your eyes. Take a look around your house. You may wish you were staring at a remodeled kitchen or new furniture, but it's what you *do* see—the clutter and ambiguous spaces—that stands between the home you have and the one you dream about.

Your first response to the state of your house might be to avert your eyes, grab your laptop, and start mindlessly scrolling through Facebook or Pinterest. Pretty soon you are cracking up from funny animal videos, daydreaming as you pin pictures of clean houses to your "I'm Going to Do This" Pinterest board, or consoling yourself with a thumbs up on a Facebook post by someone who is feeling equally overwhelmed.

When we do this, perhaps we are subconsciously searching for affirmation, direction, connection, or simply distraction from what we should be doing. I have felt the pull of those diversions many times! Yet after I scroll through a million loud conversations between people setting standards I don't have the energy to achieve, I feel more frazzled and less content than I did before.

Facing the mess we are in, understanding how we arrived here, and making a plan to deal with it are important steps toward loving the home we have. My most popular blog posts on The Inspired Room are usually about how to clean, declutter, organize, and find happiness at home. We all want our home to be our sanctuary, but we struggle one way or another with how to get there! Our desired destination might seem far away, but each hopeful step we take will make a difference. The journey is where so much of the contentment is found.

Room for Living

I'm guessing that most of us would be happier if we woke up tomorrow to less cluttered minds, cleaner floors and counters, organized closets and drawers, sparkling bathrooms, and tidier desks. (As long as we're dreaming, let's add a bouquet of flowers and a box of chocolates on the counter. I am never upset by those things, are you?)

We long for a sense of inner peace and calm, and we want those qualities to be reflected in our surroundings. Yet the clutter in our physical world and its soundtrack—the beeps and pings that punctuate our constant, in-process conversations—ensure the opposite. We feel overwhelmed, overstressed, and unable to focus on anything that matters to us. Living fully and creatively in the moment is difficult, if not impossible, when we're fracturing those moments by our continual multitasking.

Regardless of our personal tolerance for clutter and our choices about how much stuff we want or need in our home, we will not love the home we have until we master our messes. We need to take control of our stuff and not the other way around.

There is no room to grow in a home that has no breathing space. Clutter interferes with our focused productivity, so our anxiety and frustration increase. Let's commit to making room in our life and home for the things that matter most to us so we can experience more freedom.

But how, right? Unless you want to hire a housecleaning service or a professional organizer on a regular basis, someone who looks, sounds, and acts exactly like *you* will have to create and preserve that peaceful space. Our home reflects who we are. So it is important to explore how we want to express our priorities, style, and purpose. Taking care of our home is one of the most important ways we take care of ourselves. So let's find ways to do this that energize us and motivate us and even become sources of joy.

Getting Over the Hump of a Slump

Raise your hand if you ever watch the show *Hoarders* just to make yourself feel better about the state of your home! Your house might not be bad enough to warrant a TV producer's visit, but if it isn't reflecting what you want to see and isn't inspiring you to do the great things in life you know you want to do, now is the time to take action. Your home *can* be the calm oasis you dream about.

But if you are like me, about the time you find the motivation, you lose the energy to make it happen. That's so awesome.

In the absence of our own personal cleaning fairy or a TV crew to ignite our efforts, we need a boost of inspiration to start with a bang. I do what most reasonable people would do when they have no idea what to do next. No, I don't take a nap. I throw a party!

If your house is a wreck right now, I know what you're thinking—that's a completely ridiculous idea. It's unrealistic. Maybe you're squinting your eyes at me right now and scowling, thinking I've lost my mind. Why would anyone who needs to declutter her house want to stress herself out even more by throwing a party?

It's simple, my dear—I'm in control of the party date. See where I'm headed here? This, my friend, is how I motivate myself when I feel overwhelmed with all the clutter that's standing between me and my dreams. It might seem a little wacky, but somehow it works for me.

Over the years I have found that inviting others to simple gatherings at my house is the perfect motivator for me to get a jump start on things that need to happen. Perhaps you should plan a party too! I'm not suggesting you throw a theme party or black-tie event. Invite a few people over to play scrabble and eat takeout pizza if that's all you want or need to start with. Choose any event or guest that will motivate you to make progress at home without tipping you over the edge and stealing your will to live. A party might help push us into the deep end, where we sink or swim. Hopefully, we'll swim.

When I set a deadline for myself, I get inspired to accomplish things I've always wanted to do and never seem to have time for. I'm suddenly able to finish random projects like hanging pictures on the wall (the ones that sat on my floor collecting dust for years because I couldn't decide on the perfect spot for them). Each time, I'm reminded that most of the tasks I delay doing only take a few minutes to accomplish, and I wonder why I put them off for so long.

Your Invitation to Motivation

Inviting others over allows us to practice hospitality. And a welcome side benefit is that it helps us focus on the most doable, pressing tasks around the house. When no one is invited over, I feel like there is too much to do, so I end up doing hardly any of it. I just sit there in the mess.

Yet with only a few weeks or days to get things done, the goal is clearly set in front of me, and I am motivated to get busy. Usually the long-avoided chores are taken care of so simply, I am delighted, not stressed, as I check more things off my to-do list!

Now, occasionally this "party till I drop" plan backfires and I get too ambitious for my own good. One thing leads to another, and pretty soon I'm redecorating or otherwise distracted by my newfound enthusiasm. As a visual person, I can find myself dreaming of painting the dining room, for instance, just days before guests arrive for dinner. Yes, I'm ridiculous. Instead of cleaning the living room or marinating roasts the way normal people would do before guests come over, I head off to buy paint, tear apart the dining room, and move tables and chairs into another room of the house.

That means my kitchen floors may not get clean because the thought of a freshly painted dining room lured me away from scrubbing the floors. But at least the dining room is partially painted, right?

I might make insane choices prior to hosting guests, but a set party date moves me toward progress. That's the point. And since I'm prone to procrastination, I'm happy with that form of motivation. My fear of once again playing hide-and-seek underneath my table while guests knock on the door motivates me to do something. Anything. Slowly my home starts to look the way I had wanted it to all along. That's the beauty of this idea. It gets me out of my slump. And best of all, it helps me to see my house in a new light. (Never mind that I had to bag a bunch of clutter and hide it in the car trunk to meet my deadline. We can talk about that later.)

Once the guests arrive, I'm happy because the jump start gives me hope and confidence that I'm headed in a positive direction. Winning. Amazing what a little pre-party cleanup can do for our disposition and motivation! Lo and behold, my home isn't nearly as awful as I thought it was. I actually *can* enjoy the peaceful retreat I've dreamed of. I might even set a bouquet on the table and light a candle. Who knew that a party could make me feel so much better about the state of my home?

In fact, I'm so pleased with my progress, I do the unthinkable. I plan another soiree. The more people we invite over, the cleaner our house gets. And after those guests leave, even with a few dishes to wash, I get to enjoy living in a cleaner and prettier home.

Maybe seeing your house a little shinier will give you hope too. As the house becomes cleaner and you become more hospitable, you might be inspired to do more. Over time you can dig a little deeper in the nooks and crannies so you can give your home and soul what they really need—more space to breathe.

That first step of visualizing your home as a peaceful sanctuary will inspire you to continue the process. It is a gift you give yourself.

So who are you going to invite over? Let's get this party started.

Goodbye Excess, Hello Success

The first step to a clutter-free home isn't to organize the clutter into neat little color-coded bins and folders. I'm sorry to disappoint you if you were ready to head to the store for pretty containers. Organizing clutter isn't really necessary. You can try, but chances are, you'll realize two days later that you have wasted precious hours of your life on tasks that didn't improve the quality of your life. Getting rid of excess is really the only way to make room for living.

Decluttering is the best route to a more peaceful home. Removing excess anything from your home frees you from what weighs you down and creates more space for what you really want in your life.

By letting go of things that are taking up valuable space in your home, you will be inspired to live more simply. With less stuff, you can more easily organize what you do use. You can stop shuffling clutter from room to room. And you can be deliberate about what you bring into your home so you live with only the things you love and need around you.

Shelf-Discipline

I had a small craft room in the castle. It was actually a safe room because it had a steel door and a lock, but we used it to store all our craft supplies. Anytime my kids had a school project or I got inspired to make something crafty, we could find what we needed in only a few moments. Contrary to the popular notion about creative people being messy, I experience pure bliss when I have order in the craft room. Knowing I can find the scissors, grab the polka-dot ribbon, or locate the poster board makes me less frazzled and much more inspired.

During the first few years in our new house, we had an open shelving unit for crafts in our TV room. Unfortunately, the shelving unit was ill-equipped for the types of craft materials we had. It was pretty much a disaster. Anytime we needed a certain type of paint, paper, or other creative supply, we wouldn't be able to find it. Stuff was piled high and would get more and more disorganized as we shuffled through boxes and bags. There was no way to organize it all effectively. We finally stopped even looking on the shelves because it was easier to buy something new.

Eventually we knew that cycle needed to end. That shelf became a symbol of a cluttered mind, not a creative opportunity. It held us back from enjoying the room because every time we saw the shelf, we were reminded how disorganized we were. The only way to stop the madness was to get rid of almost all the craft items (we donated them to our church) and dismantle the shelves.

To preserve our sanity, we had to start over with a clean slate. Why did we keep something around for so long that added frustration to our lives? Partly because we had no idea how creatively freeing it would

Pruning the EXCESS —EVEN THE good STUFF— MAKES room FOR A MORE creative & fulfilling life

be to remove that sore spot. Once the shelving was no longer in the room, we were inspired to hang a gallery of family photos in its place. We added a bookcase to the corner for my husband's books. Now he is more inspired to study and write. Every time we walk by that space, we feel inspired and relieved. Goodbye overwhelmed.

Pruning the excess, even the good stuff, makes room for a more creative and fulfilling life. When we let the clutter multiply around us, we don't know when to say yes to something new, when to say no to something we don't need, or how to let go of what we have. We become managers of things, shufflers of papers, searchers of lost keys. We are anxious instead of peaceful. We waste hours of our lives on things that don't matter to us, and we have no time to make our home a launching pad for our family's dreams and goals.

Rooms Are for Living

When we realized that the living room in our new house wasn't being used much, we knew that we needed to empty the space of everything so we could see it in a new light. Once the room was free of clutter, we immediately saw its creative potential. The ideas and possibilities had room to take shape. We created that open canvas where we could visualize dreams and identify what we wanted and needed. By emptying out a space, you are inviting in creative ideas for how to use and love the home you have. I do this same exercise with every room I need to declutter.

When my office gets out of control, I gather all the papers and random items that land there and move them out of that space. Instantly, my office and mind breathe a sigh of relief. Then I'm inspired to bring back in only what I really need. If you do this with every room in your home over time, you will discover what a gift it is to envision your spaces differently, remove the daily debris, and look forward to the transformation.

Making room for what we want will inspire us to be focused editors of our belongings so we will add back in only those things that serve us and our home's purpose.

Create a Clutter-Free Destination

I like to designate a purpose for each and every corner of my home. I've found it helpful to first break each room into several mini-destinations and then name each one for its unique purpose.

When I define the use for a space, I can more easily create a design that is both pretty and functional. Also, when we dedicate a corner for a specific purpose, my family and I are more likely to maintain it as a tidy and pleasant destination.

For greatest success, I pinpoint a need we have for more function or beauty—a problem we need to solve—and then I identify solutions that make the most sense for us. Over time, I consider each corner, one by one, throughout our entire house.

We've set up destination corners for my husband to play the guitar and study and for my son to play his games. We've arranged an outdoor office and a fire pit area for family fun. We have a destination for me to write, an area in our kitchen for baking, a coffee station where friends can gather, and even a quiet corner by the fireplace for quiet reflection and prayer.

Setting up destinations is a great way to get rid of clutter! You will be motivated to clear out excess to make way for them. Sometimes all the clutter ends up in another room as the rest of the house takes shape, and that's okay if you have the space and aren't able to get rid of everything yet. Don't be too hard on yourself or expect miracles overnight. It might take some time to let go of the clutter once and for all.

Let only one room or one corner of the garage be the sorting station, and don't let your stuff re-invade an area already set up as a destination. Gradually you can make your way setting up destinations around the entire house. Finally even the clutter in your holding room will get the boot, and that room will get a brand-new purpose.

Peaceful Corners

One corner in our gathering room (a.k.a. living room) became a reading-corner destination. First we pinpointed our need within the

Setting Up a Decluttered Destination

- Identify a specific need or a purpose for the destination.
- Give clutter the boot and be inspired by a blank slate!
- Identify the past problems with the space.
- Solve the problems by incorporating beautiful and useful items.
- Enjoy the beauty of a decluttered space.
- Be inspired to keep it clutter free!

larger space. In this case, we wanted a place to display our books and a comfortable nook for reading. Our next step was to give unused items away so a blank slate could inspire us. We then identified some of the problems we had in the past with this space. For example, the dogs run through this area all the time, stirring up dust bunnies. It was also used as a dumping area where we would leave books and bags and everything else as we came in the front door. The size of the area was limited, and it needed specific-sized furniture.

We saved up to make the changes and add functional, attractive furniture. A dust-free glass cabinet for our books and a comfortable settee for reading were just right. The results were worth the wait. Now when we walk through the room, it invites us in to pick up a book and relax. Even if we don't have time to sit down right then, the peace of the corner invites us to slow down and breathe. It reminds us of the life we want to live.

When a space is designed with a purpose, we are less likely to fill it with clutter that looks out of place and disturbs the peace. Priorities help establish purpose, and purpose helps maintain priorities. Big win.

What type of destinations could you create in your home? Pick one and get started!

A Home for Everything

As you remove everything from a destination, put back only what you actually need there. And don't just put it back—give each item or type of item a designated home.

You've probably heard the expression "a place for everything and everything in its place." When everything you need is in its designated spot, it's so much easier to keep up your systems and determine which items are essential and which are unnecessary.

Now, let me clarify that I'm not a highly detailed organizer. I tend to get overwhelmed if there are too many colored-coded systems and a labeled bin (with a detailed list of contents) for every item in my entire home. I went through a phase in my earlier homemaking life when I had three-by-five cards to list every item in the boxes we stored in our attic. It was inspiring for a year or so, but eventually it just annoyed me because it was one more thing I had to keep up with and one more system that could fall apart.

If you've got the time and mindset for that level of detailed organization, go for it! But my personal experience is that if I get too detailed or rigid, I'll lose steam and eventually lose interest in using the system. But if everything has a home base, I'm more effective and productive with my day, and my house is functional and orderly.

I feel organized when I can find what I need in my house in five minutes or less. That means each area must be (essentially) clutter free, every functional destination in our home needs to be identified, and our process needs to make sense to us so we can easily navigate our home and maintain our favorite systems.

Make It Happen

What destination would inspire you the most? *A reading corner? A coffee station? A command center for decluttering papers and reminders? Start with the one that sounds the most doable, fun, or rewarding.*

Set a goal for when you want this space to be complete.

What is your biggest motivation for decluttering? *Space? Beauty? Peace? Freedom to entertain on a whim?*

CHAPTER 7

The Reward of Daily Routines

*What you do every day matters more than
what you do once in a while.*
GRETCHEN RUBIN

I love the idea of a clean house. I love the idea of an organized house. I love the idea of figuring out how to maintain my house so it looks pretty good most of the time. Those desires motivate me long enough to plan a party or clean a room, but they aren't quite enough to keep me on track. There are just too many other distractions every day. (Look—squirrel! Shiny things!)

I am prone to start a housekeeping project and end up with a bigger mess. Or I end up shopping or rearranging furniture instead of cleaning. I have trouble focusing on tasks, and the ones that have to do with cleaning don't rise to the top of my fun list.

I like to say that I'm too busy with work and family priorities to be tidy, but my husband points out that when he first met me, my room was a disaster. I was a teenager, and I thought that was a great excuse not to be a clean freak. I think I have outgrown that excuse and any grace tied to it.

We make time for the things we want to do, so it's pretty clear where my priorities have *not* been all my life. Don't get me wrong—I definitely want the clean house. I just wish someone else would do it for me.

I would still be wallowing in excuses if I hadn't found a creative way around my flightiness. It's safe to say I wasn't born with the housekeeping gene. I was born a dreamer. People like me should be automatically gifted with a housekeeper—or even better, a full-time staff to go along with the big dreams. But in the absence of those helps, I have to get in the right frame of mind to keep up with housekeeping.

I finally realized I needed to turn my desire for a beautiful house into motivation to follow daily routines that would transform my home (without me realizing what was happening).

Perhaps my simple tricks will inspire you as they have inspired me. Or if you were born with the organization gene, maybe they'll amuse you.

Developing Home Habits

Hosting a party motivates me to clean, and arranging corner destinations prompts me to clear clutter, so naturally I needed a creative motivation to override my natural inclination to find something more fun to do than housework (and what isn't?). A long time ago, I realized I needed to develop my own home habits. But getting into habits wasn't easy for me!

I tried the various chore charts and calendars suggested by experts, but it turns out I had more fun making the colorful task grids and placing them in pretty notebooks than I did implementing a plan.

When faced with a complicated cleaning schedule, I am incapable of getting past the second day of assignments. I wasn't born yesterday—no one (not even me) can trick me into following a weekly chart. I resist the obligation to clean toilets on Tuesdays. In fact, I would probably clean my toilet on Monday just to break the rules, and then I'd throw off the entire week. My rebellion against following someone else's structure for my day might also explain why I eventually became self-employed. I guess I'm a free spirit—if I have to clean, I'm going to do it according to my whims.

Over the years I've read many websites and books that offered hope that I could overcome my crazy issues. I learned the importance of routine though Flylady.net. I laughed my way through *Sidetracked Home*

Executives and felt a kindred connection with Alexandra Stoddard in *Living a Beautiful Life*. I related to both of those books even though they are so different. That confession probably sheds light on why I needed to come up with my own way of loving the home I have. (It could also reveal a split-personality disorder.)

Eventually, I had to set aside any one specific model, embrace my sidetracked ways, gather my dreams and motivations for a beautiful life, and develop my personal home habits.

The good news is that after learning from other people's experiences and mixing in my creativity and beauty preferences, I have established a few daily rhythms that I have found helpful and actually enjoyed for years now.

My daily routines motivate me, they remind me to do the next task, and they even reward me for my effort. They have become a part of life that I really look forward to, and when I don't do them, I feel like my day is incomplete. There is hope in habits!

The Freedom of Routines

I'm easily overwhelmed by options. I can't even decide what to order for dinner at restaurants. So when I had a houseful of small children and pets, I was too overwhelmed to find a starting place. It wasn't that I didn't want to clean behind the toilets and dust behind dressers and reorganize desk drawers. I did. I do. I believe in those things. I want those things to happen. I'm pro-cleaning. My problem was, and can still be, the combination of high expectations and low ability to make it all happen.

I was a pro procrastinator. If I couldn't get everything done in one inspired round of cleaning, I figured, why bother starting? I wanted to see an immediate reward for my efforts. But without enough time, desire, or coffee in a day to power through the full six-page list of chores, I'd have to wait far too long to see the reward. Like eternity.

Then I had an epiphany. What if I didn't expect myself to do everything on my housekeeping list right now, or even at all? What if I only had to do a few important things every day? What if I chose tasks that offered immediate rewards? These questions helped me recognize that I'd have to let some things go to save my sanity and to focus on what I could do consistently.

Out of that season of questions, I came up with my answer—four simple routines. Not ten, not fifteen. Not a binder packed with color-coded options. Not a different routine for every day of the week. I thought I was a bit crazy to aim for that low number, but over the years, I've shared my four daily routines with hundreds of thousands of women online. I've received countless emails from women who are enjoying their days again because they aren't struggling to keep up with complicated chore charts and expectations. They can finally love their homes.

Pretending we don't care about housekeeping is trendy, but most of us really do care. Still, we swing back and forth between the two perspectives.

- We live here—therefore our house is a mess.
- We live here—therefore we don't want it to be a mess.

The trick is to find simple ways to reduce the mess so our homes can be pleasant places to live. Daily routines keep me from slipping into the lonely abyss of despair when I'm insanely busy. I know I can keep up with a few things every day. I can always do more, but it's so nice to have realistic expectations.

The Four Routines

My routines are not rocket science. Women have been doing them to complement their housekeeping process for years! But I believe this simple combination is enjoyable, doable, and effective. The result is a mini-miracle. I get twice as much done and feel twice as encouraged when I follow through. Here are my four daily routines that offer the hope of a clean house:

1. morning routine
2. sink scrubbings

3. cleaning frenzies

4. evening routine

1. Morning Routine

My morning mindset improves when I have something to look forward to as soon as I open my eyes. Like coffee! I love the smell of it. I love the ritual of pouring a cup and sipping as the steam rises. I don't even drink that much, but I *enjoy* coffee as a part of my routine. A simple morning routine can be as quick as ten to thirty minutes or as long as an hour or two.

Adjust the routines to be realistic for your typical day. And whatever you do, don't make excuses for why you can't have a morning routine, even if you just get dressed, brush your teeth, wipe out your sink, and throw the covers over your bed. That is a morning routine most everyone can manage and benefit from.

Don't be discouraged if it doesn't feel natural right away—it takes at least a month to form the habit. Soon you'll start to look forward to your routine! Your day will be less stressful, and your home will be more in order! When I first started my morning routines and kept them for longer than a week, my husband questioned whether I was the same woman he married.

Making the Case for Making Your Bed

Make your bed. It's good for you. Okay, I just risked sounding like your camp counselor or (oh, no) your mother because I believe this one teensy task can transform your life. And I'm not the only one who thinks so.

In the book *The Power of Habit*, author Charles Duhigg suggests that such routines as making your bed every day, exercising, and cooking are called keystone habits.[3] Keystone habits are routines that inspire other good habits. Once a daily routine becomes second nature, it becomes an effortless and rewarding part of your day. Once you master a keystone habit, you'll add other new, good habits into your life. It certainly has been true in my case.

I understand asking, why make a bed when I just undo it at the end of the day? I lived by that logic for many years. But I'll tell you this much—once I added making the bed to my morning routine, everything about my day started to change!

The first thing I noticed was my sense of accomplishment in having completed a task first thing in the morning. As I smoothed my sheets, pulled up the comforter, and set out the pillow shams and throw pillows, I stepped back to admire my work. That simple ritual reminded me to open my blinds so the sun would filter in and shine on that lovely bed. I walked away from the bedroom (looking back for one final sigh of contentment with my accomplishment so early in the morning) feeling empowered to tackle the day.

As the day went on, I was less likely to pile belongings on the bed. (I was definitely less likely to crawl back under the covers midday.) I didn't worry that when the kids or dogs jumped across the bed they'd leave crumbs or toys in my sheets, making my return to those sheets less than enjoyable. I was more content every time I walked through my room and saw evidence of beauty and order. The tidy bed also inspired me to add to my evening routine by turning on the nightstand lamps and sometimes neatly turning down the covers to create a cozy ambience for the day's end.

I was more likely to wash my sheets regularly so they felt and smelled fresh when I turned down the bed and crawled in at night. I started to

Style Notes

On vacation, don't you love entering your hotel room after housekeepers have made your bed? I feel cared for and encouraged by such an inviting, relaxing scene. Decide which simple actions suit your lifestyle and make yourself and your family feel cared for—those will become the best of habits.

Two Essentials for a Morning Routine

1. Make a list of the minimum tasks you need to complete every morning to feel productive, pulled together, energized, and ready to dive into the day's work (for example, brush your teeth, make the bed, shower, get dressed, unload the dishwasher, or have some quiet time). Commit to doing your designated tasks every morning.

2. Throw in an activity or two you enjoy or that will inspire your morning (such as having coffee, playing music, journaling, reading the Bible, praying, walking, or catching up on blogs). These simple pleasures will make your morning routine something to look forward to, so do them every morning as your treat to yourself.

free the floor and nightstands of clutter. Our room became our sanctuary, and we treated it as our retreat.

If the few moments it takes to make a bed will also make us happier and more productive, I'd say it's time well spent! Give bed making a try as a part of your morning routine and let me know how it enhances your day.

After you create your morning routine, post it on your mirror until it becomes a habit.

2. Sink Scrubbings

My mom taught my sister and me to appreciate clean sinks. Her friends always asked her how she managed to keep our bathroom and kitchen sinks so shiny. Her secret was so simple! When she was done with whatever she was doing—brushing her teeth or scrubbing pans—she rinsed the sink and then polished it with a rag she kept in the cupboard beneath. Who knew that the elimination of toothpaste residue or clumps of dried oatmeal could make such a difference? Yet this simple habit will transform a kitchen or bathroom. Daily housekeeping habits become like dominoes—one successful task leads to the next!

You won't even want to stack dishes in your beautiful kitchen sink because of your shiny new habit. Make a commitment to keep those sinks clean all day, every day! As a reminder, you can post a note above the faucets until this routine sinks in. (See what I did there?)

HOUSEKEEPING
Daily Habits
BECOME LIKE
DOMINOES
ONE *successful* TASK *leads* TO THE *next*

3. Cleaning Frenzies

Since our early years of marriage, my husband and I have utilized what we affectionately call a "cleaning frenzy" to give our home a quick makeover during the day. A frenzy can last ten minutes or a full hour. We like to do at least one a day—two is even better. Everyone can participate, including the kids. We run around picking things up from the floor, putting items away, and making everything tidy. You can get into a cleaning frenzy all on your own too, but they do tend to be contagious!

Sometimes we focus on one room, but when we have a burst of energy or some extra time, we run around the entire house picking up clutter. Frenzies work like a charm to make a big impact in a short period of time.

To spark your creativity, here are brief descriptions of four different frenzies. These cleaning blitzes are very easy to adapt to your unique needs and your home's purpose. I truly believe that a ten-minute cleaning frenzy a day keeps the housekeeping frustration away. Set one a day as a goal, and if you can do a few more, go for it. They are fun!

Horizontal Surface Frenzy

Clean one horizontal surface or as many as you can in ten minutes! This is where most of us gather our clutter. Look at the kitchen counter, bedroom nightstand, coffee table, dining table, stovetop, or the floor of any room and choose your frenzy focus. Any surface of any room will do! Take everything off the surface, wipe it down, dust or vacuum it, and put back only what is truly useful or beautiful for that space.

Find a home for the clutter you removed. Make it your goal going forward to keep that area decluttered and clean!

Vertical Surface Frenzy

With ten minutes on the timer, you can polish up a lot of vertical surfaces. Focus a cleaning frenzy on light-switch plates, doorknobs, windows, mirrors, doors, backsplashes, lamp bases and shades, accessories, or picture frames.

Bathroom Cleaning Frenzy

Unless your house is a mansion, you should be able to clean all your toilets in ten minutes or less. Grab your cleanser, a cleaning wand, and a rag and get scrubbing! Disinfect and polish inside and out. Get into a cleaning frenzy with bathroom counters, showers, floors, and cabinets!

Laundry Frenzy

The best way to keep up with laundry is to do it every day. If this isn't possible, do laundry frenzies as often as you can throughout the week. Toss a load in and set a timer so you remember to move clothes to the dryer. Immediately hang or lay out dry or almost-dry clothes to prevent wrinkles. With another ten-minute block, you can put away clothes or have other family members join in a quick frenzy to retrieve their items and put them away by the end of the day.

4. Evening Routine

After a long day, right before bedtime, the last thing I want to do is face a long list of cleaning expectations. So I keep my nightly routine simple. Your evening routine might include making dinner, helping kids with homework, running baths, and catching up on communication or work to prepare for the next morning. Responsibilities can take over our evening, so it's important to relax. Following a manageable evening routine can help you create the emotional and physical space to breathe.

We clean the kitchen as our nightly routine. Before bed, we run the final dishwasher load of the day, wipe off counters, and polish the sink before we turn out the lights. Believe me, walking into your tidy kitchen for that first cup of coffee is a peaceful way to begin your day.

If your kitchen doesn't get a lot of use during the day, consider another evening task that brings order to your home. Folding and putting away laundry can be relaxing and will help you and your family find something to wear when the morning alarm goes off.

There are many little rituals we can use to enhance our experience every day at home. In the upcoming chapters, I will share many more of my favorite routines and the simple ways I fall in love with my home. Regardless of where you live or what kind of craziness is going on around you, the daily gifts you give yourself and the routines you practice in your life can transform your house into a home.

Get Inspired

Look around your house. What are three cleaning, clearing, or organizing tasks that could make a big difference in how your home feels? *How could you work those into a daily routine?*

What form of support has helped you make and keep good habits in other areas of life (an accountability partner, rewards, to-do lists, before and after photos, progress charts...)? *Choose a method or two to inspire your commitment to new daily routines.*

Consider writing down your daily routines to keep you focused and motivated. *As a little gift for you, I've created a lovely printable sheet you can download for free. Come over to lovethehomeyouhave.com and print it out.*

CHAPTER 8

The Clean-Enough House

*My second favorite household chore is ironing. My first being
hitting my head on the top bunk bed until I faint.*
ERMA BOMBECK

We can easily feel paralyzed when the house is out of control, can't we? I remember many times wanting to toss my entire house into a giant dumpster and start over. But now that I have determined the purpose for my home, set some realistic goals, and eased into my four easy daily routines, I have discovered some gentle ways to find my way through the chaos. These guidelines help me stay on the right track to do exactly what I need to be doing at this time and in this place. My daily routines have transformed my life, bolstering my confidence to chase my dreams and helping me find time to embrace my purpose.

But there are still those days when I look around and have a sinking feeling that I haven't done enough. Does a stern voice in your head ever say you couldn't possibly do enough to keep up? When this happens (and chances are, it will), take a deep breath and tell yourself...

"My house is clean enough."

I have often needed to repeat those words over the years. With a husband, babies, and small children to love, a super-clean house was not my top priority. Even with Cheerios and toys everywhere, my house *was* clean enough in those days because my babies needed my attention and my husband wanted a date night now and then in front of the TV. I don't regret the hours I set the housekeeping aside so I could embrace my family.

Even now, when my office is currently surrounded by more clutter and disarray than I want to see, my house is clean enough for this moment. We've been painting inside, so our furniture pieces are scattered in rooms where they don't belong. And to top it off, our water heater is broken. The plumbers are running around our house, trying not to trip on our stuff. I'm cringing at the chaos the plumbers have witnessed. Am I happy with this level of disarray? No. But it is what it is.

In our defense, my family hasn't been able to do dishes, wash clothes, or take showers for days. It's hot outside. Our house stinks. We stink. Our routines are off. Dishes are on the counter. Laundry is piling up on the floor. We are trying to do many things and dropping the ball on most of them. Pretty soon this plumber will hand us a $3000 bill for a new water heater and repairs. As I write a check for that painful amount, I will be reminded why we work and don't have time to clean house all day.

So here I am thinking it again: Our house is clean enough. I can restart the routines tomorrow. All things considered, life is good. We are grateful we will soon have a water heater. We'll have water! That's a gift. I don't need to carry the burden that I haven't done enough yet—today is a day for grace. And maybe a cookie. Definitely a cookie.

Friend, when your day sounds like mine, when you're running around doing your best while everything seems to be falling apart around you, go put your feet up and remind yourself that tomorrow is a new day. Tomorrow you can get back to your routines and maybe do an extra cleaning frenzy to make up for everything that fell apart today. Today your house is clean enough.

Be Realistic

No one will ever be able to do it all. We know this, so it's kind of crazy to think we will be the first to succeed. But we can do enough.

The trick is to figure out what "enough" means for us. There aren't any one-size-fits-all requirements for housekeeping because we all live with different circumstances and preferences. Many years ago I decided I could cope with my own standards and my ever-fluctuating circumstances if I gave myself permission to define a clean-enough house. In order to know what this means to me today or this week, I visualize a goal and fill in the blank.

I want my house to be clean enough to...

_____.

I can adapt that statement every day if I want to. Here are a few ways I have applied it lately:

- I want my dining-room table to be clean enough to eat dinner on tonight.
- I want my house to be clean enough to invite someone over.
- I want my kitchen clean and sparkling so I come home to order after a busy Monday.

I'll be honest—on some days I just want my house clean enough for me to carry a laundry basket through our TV room and not end up in traction with a broken leg. And there are evenings when I am so tired, I acknowledge the many important things I took care of instead of cleaning that day...and then I go to bed.

Realistically, the condition of my home will vary daily depending on what's going on. But I strive to keep up with the routines even when the state of my house threatens to take over my day or mess with my emotional health. I can always do more, but at least I can cover the basics.

Both of my daughters have been personal assistants to busy and productive women. These women identified their top stressor as "being overwhelmed by disorder," and they wanted help straightening up their homes. They dreamed of clean sinks, tidy surfaces, made beds, folded clothes, and maybe even a bouquet on the counter.

— Style Notes —

Want to fly through your cleaning routine? What we wear can affect our efficiency! Sorry to disappoint you (and me), but PJs tell us to be lazy and maybe even crawl back in bed. Getting dressed tells us to get busy.

Super-nice clothes tell me I shouldn't clean at all. Aprons tell me it is okay to tackle a quick cleaning job regardless of what I'm wearing. Moral of this—get dressed, and I bet you'll be more efficient. Try it!

Most of us are encouraged and inspired by a pleasantly clean and tidy house whether we work in or out of the home. We don't want to obsess over cleanliness, but we do need to make basic routines a priority in our lives for our own good. Creating a happy home can be a part of our day.

Let's make housekeeping as simple as possible. We can't spend all day cleaning or trying to keep up with lofty expectations. I have a life to live, and so do you. I truly believe that if we simplify our expectations we will thrive and be able to accomplish what we want.

Remember your priorities so you can be realistic about what "clean enough" means for you. If your priorities are to raise and nurture your young family, you know that beautiful messes will happen daily in this season of your life. Embrace them! If you are building a career, recognize that you won't have much time to invest in your home. If you are serving others and impacting the world, your daily routines will give you the energy and motivation to keep on being your awesome self! A clean-enough house empowers us to *be more*—while doing less to stay ahead of the chaos.

Be Consistent

The key to successful housekeeping is to turn daily routines into doable habits so you have time to enjoy the fruit of your labor. When you experience a clean-enough house for a couple months in a row, you'll be inspired to keep up the momentum and envision new possibilities for your home and life!

You'll feel better and more in control after each little housekeeping win! Every time you make the bed, you'll be pleased to see it as you pass by. Every day you polish up your sink, you'll be happier. Those are little victories. And consistent little victories add up to the bigger win, which starts to unfold after you've been doing your routines for a month.

Consistency with daily cleaning frenzies is one of the secrets to a clean-enough house. We can do them anytime we have a few moments.

A clean-enough HOUSE EMPOWERS US TO be more WHILE doing less TO STAY AHEAD OF THE CHAOS

Instead of wasting ten minutes surfing the Internet or staring into space listening to elevator music while on hold with the repair people, we can put those moments to good use and get into a little frenzy.

Whenever our house starts to get a little crazy (it happens), we know it's time for a cleaning frenzy! We pause our other activities, pump up the tunes, and put stuff away. A lot gets done in a few minutes. If we have 30 minutes or an hour, that's a bonus!

Cleaning frenzies are simple to gear up for, and they can be very contagious! When you see someone improving one part of the house, you just can't help yourself. And even if others don't share your initial enthusiasm, they will soon learn that when the timer comes out and the tunes go on, it's time to get into the groove.

Pretty soon everyone is washing dishes, clearing surfaces, and finding homes for stray items. Before you know it, the house is cleaner than moments before. You can step back and smile at a tidier room. And the frenzy participants will be amazed at how easy it was to clean it up and make it better than it was. You just had to get started!

Once you've tried cleaning frenzies for 30 days in a row, strange things will begin to appear, like the tops of dressers and cabinets. And you'll be so happy about the state of your house, you'll want to preserve the new look! It's the consistency that makes the difference over the long term. Your home is going to be pretty amazing!

I've been doing this in my house for many years now, and I can say with confidence that it was the consistency of my effort that paid off the most. When you adopt the clean-enough house principle, you'll receive two huge rewards—permission to be content with doing enough, and the clear path to new adventures that might come your way on any given day!

If you are sitting within view of a mess (ahem), maybe you should get into a cleaning frenzy. It may not solve every problem around you, but it will make a difference, one little frenzy at a time. In fact, let's do this together, shall we? I bet we all have a mess somewhere that needs help. I know I do.

Here is the mission. Let's all put on our favorite 1980s tunes, set a timer for ten minutes, pick a room, and GO FOR IT! Remember, a few frenzies a day keep the crazies away.

Be Ready for the Day

Some nights I am wiped out and want to go to bed without doing everything in my nightly routine. Maybe I'll want to skip tidying the kitchen. No big deal, I deserve a break. But once I start negotiating which parts of my routine to do or not do, it's hard to get back on track. Pretty soon I'm shortchanging every night's simple plan, and I'm bummed in the mornings because I start out behind.

The truth is, I always feel as if I deserve to go to bed without doing dishes! I mean, honestly. Dishes? Or bed? Bed will always win if given a chance. But after doing my routines all these years, I know I feel best when I can get out of bed ready to start the day. I don't know about you, but if I have to face dirty dishes in the morning, 20 extra minutes of sleep won't motivate me to leap out of bed smiling (or at all, for that matter).

Reframing the Reward

When I'm tempted to put off until tomorrow the tasks I could manage to do now, I ask myself this: Do I deserve to wake up to a clean kitchen tomorrow? Yes. Yes I do. I might be entitled to watch a show before bed. I might need a little extra sleep. Those are rewards after a long day. Doing the dishes might seem like a chore, but when I remember the reward of starting tomorrow ready for the day rather than behind, I'm more likely to stay on course and finish out the evening with my routines. Yes, I deserve to wake up to a clean kitchen, and so do you.

Every day is filled with new and exciting opportunities, and we don't want to miss out on them just because we are stuck in the kitchen scraping the remnants of last night's lasagna out of pans. As you probably gathered from my stories, when I was a young wife, I worried that someone would come by our house unannounced. I wasn't a fan of drop-in visitors because they interrupted my day, and

I wasn't organized enough to be prepared for unannounced visits. I still consider my home my sanctuary, and I want to be able to enjoy the peace of that refuge, but I also want to be available, gracious, and welcoming when opportunity knocks.

When I do my routines, I am more prepared and far more open to little divine interruptions. I don't want to look back on life and see myself hiding under a table instead of talking to a dear friend, a new friend, or a person in need of a listening ear. The rewards for being ready can be life changing.

Waking up and starting the day by making the bed, raising the blinds, tossing in some laundry, brewing my cup of coffee, jumping in the shower...that's a comforting routine for me. I start out the day with confidence. My house is clean enough, so I'm ready for whatever the day brings.

My husband knows I like to take a shower and get dressed as soon as I wake up. I've done that since we were first married. Even when my kids were small and we had to drive them to school, I did my best to not drive them in my jammies. I wasn't always successful, but it was an honorable goal.

Taking a shower, getting dressed, putting on my makeup, and doing my hair are important parts of every morning for me. They're in my routine. I feel more prepared to take care of my home and accomplish my work when I'm fully dressed.

I'm not the only benefactor of this plan. It is also a gift to my husband, who also works from home. He doesn't have to see me walking around all day with bed-head and with drool marks on my chin. Just as a clean-enough home prepares me for whatever the day brings, I consider it a blessing to myself and my family to make sure I'm cleaned up and ready for my day.

Clean As You Go

In spite of my best efforts to keep a daily routine, sometimes things go a little wonky and I lose control of the house. I'm sure you can relate. It happens to all of us!

Sometimes houses get messy because we have too much stuff and we don't know where to put it. Living areas get messy because we don't feel like putting things away after we've used them. Kitchens become messy because someone wants to eat again. (Seriously, why does it seem like people want to eat EVERY DAY? Sigh.) Or every corner is unruly because we have kids or dogs or a family. For whatever reasons, we lose control and our house threatens to win the battle.

But not to fear—your daily routines aren't failing you. The feeling of being out of control is simply a reminder to employ a little more intentional effort throughout the day. Realizing the need for a little more effort is a good thing. One of our biggest wins around our house was discovering the simple principle of cleaning as you go. Believe it or not, the order in which you do your cleaning changes the outcome of your day in many ways. I resisted the idea for a long time, but giving it a try eventually changed our life for the better.

By cleaning as you go and intercepting small piles before they grow into time-consuming messes, you'll save yourself tons of effort and stress each day—especially over the course of a month. You'll discover the discipline and rhythm you need to create more of what you want for your day, and you'll spend less effort on the things you don't want.

My simple, clean-as-you-go tips can save you hours over the course of your week, and you'll be much less frustrated every month when you look around your home and realize you've made real progress. While it might take a bit of time to get used to incorporating these small steps into your day, your motivation will increase as you see the results. You'll feel as if your house is almost always clean enough, and you'll be ready and energized to tackle each day.

Clean-As-You-Go Tips

- Clean up the shower while you are taking a shower.

- Wipe out the sink after you brush your teeth.

- Do laundry every day instead of once a week.

- Throw all the laundry in the wash before you start breakfast.

- Pull clothes out of the dryer and hang immediately. Don't pile anything in a laundry basket but socks, undies, or towels.

- Always empty the dishwasher before you cook or eat.

- Put dirty dishes directly in the dishwasher instead of piling them in the sink. Soak and wash pots promptly after cooking.

- Clear the table right after dinner.

- Start the dishwasher right after the dinner dishes are put in.

- Clean the toilet when you have a moment or you notice it needs it. Wipe the entire thing, not just the bowl.

- Wipe off the counter before you leave the kitchen or bathroom.

- Hang up your not-yet-dirty clothes and put dirty items in the laundry bin as soon as you take them off.

- Immediately deal with anything that comes into your house. Put mail in a designated place, recycle junk mail immediately, and hang coats and backpacks on designated hooks.

- If cleaning something or putting it back in its spot will only take a couple minutes, do it right away.

If you use a system of heavy cleaning at the end of the week or a once-a-week schedule (bathrooms on Tuesday, dusting on Wednesday...), cleaning as you go might initially seem like constant cleaning. But trust me, after a month you'll adjust, and those few moments of cleaning throughout the day will get easier because you'll have developed a new habit.

Whether you grab a pair of socks off the dining table and put them in the hamper or you aim for a five-minute frenzy to tackle a toppling pile of mail, cleaning as you go rewards you with a more consistently clean-enough house. And that, in turn, prepares your home for the life you want and creates more time to spend with others.

When you adopt the clean-enough house principle, you give yourself the grace to live a full and meaningful life. Sometimes, a sink full of dishes just has to wait because you have more important tasks (or precious things, like babies!) to deal with in the moment.

Allow your home to evolve, improve, and get cleaner and more organized over time. Hang on to your sanity and humor through the process because tomorrow is a new day!

Consider This

What does "clean enough" mean to you today? *A clean-enough house empowers you to create boundaries around your free time so you can live a productive, joyful, and balanced life with the ones you love.*

How have messes kept you from doing something you wanted to do or being something you wanted to be (welcoming, peaceful, or efficient)? *Commit to keeping up with your daily routines and embracing a clean-enough house so you can live life to the full and change the world.*

What are some things you really want to do with your life? *What are your big dreams and hopes?*

CHAPTER 9

Adding Charm & Character

An interior is the natural projection of the soul.
COCO CHANEL

My favorite home store is Anthropologie. I just love walking around the store, soaking in all the charming details and marveling at their stylists' creative ingenuity in displaying merchandise and artistic elements. The store's ambience is warm, cozy, and filled with layers of character. (Okay, I actually wouldn't mind moving in!)

Through the years, my leisurely strolls through Anthropologie have inspired me to look outside the box for decorating ideas to add character to my home. They use pallets for wall shelving units, old book pages for wallpaper, tree branches to hang art...they have mastered the art of repurposing. After strolling around their displays, I've even been inspired to take a second look at items in my own house with an eye for possibility. Suddenly my antique bed, an old table, or a dated chair holds potential for charm.

Fair warning—if you stare too long at an Anthropologie catalog, you might decide you should move to an old barn and hang your chairs upside down from the ceiling as art (because really, almost anything would look amazing in a rustic barn). But don't let the lack of natural character in your normal, suburban home dull your creative sparkle.

The good news is that character isn't only found in old houses or rustic barns. Every home can be filled with charming details if you know a few of the secrets!

Reflect Your Charm and Character

I love a home that feels like a snapshot of a person's life. A place where accessories reveal stories about people's character, their travels, and what matters the most to them. I think that's why I like Anthropologie so much. It feels as if someone has traveled the world and collected a variety of mementos she found interesting, humorous, or meaningful. Even if you and I haven't traveled the world, we can gather the modern, the quirky, the reinvented, the antique, and the memorable—and let them happily coexist in one personality-filled space.

Do you embrace your own uniqueness? Do you appreciate the charm that makes you, *you*? What do you love about life? What are some of your favorite memories? Our style at home should flow out of our personality and life experiences.

I use the term "authentic style" to describe the personal, unique style we each bring to our own home. When you decorate in your authentic style, you surround yourself with things that you are passionate about and that have great meaning to your family. Your home is most charming when it reflects your heart, soul, way of living, history...everything you love.

I add some things to my home simply because they are useful. But I realize that to be fully connected to a space and drawn to spend time in a room, I need to bring in objects and elements that inspire. I add colors I love, frame cards my husband gave me, and display artwork my children made. Each piece tells a part of our story.

We have turned several walls in our home into photo galleries. They preserve wonderful memories of travel and experiences together. In our entry, we have a tray of seashells as a reminder of our many family beach trips. I've displayed a violin my grandpa gave us and teacups that remind me of my grandma. We treasure a beautiful canvas featuring the names of places around Portland (our hometown) and the Oregon

CREATE A HOME *inspired* BY YOUR *life* & WHAT YOU *love* AND THEN YOUR HOME WILL *inspire you*

coast, and we have several meaningful Bible verses painted on wood or art canvases throughout our home.

We decorate with things that transform our family on many levels. Over the years, we have collected old and new books to add color, pattern, and texture with stories we love to read and share with friends. Books add ambience and meaning to every room in our home. I love collecting beautiful cookbooks in the kitchen—they inspire me to try a new recipe, and they entice me to slow down and enjoy a feast of photos and artwork. Create a home inspired by your life and what you love, and then your home will inspire you!

A Place to Chat and Put Up Your Feet

If you can't make yourself at home in many corners of your house, you won't ever feel "at home." The charming ambience you crave is possible, regardless of what you have to work with, when you create a *comfortable place to be*. Each corner and main space can become a welcoming area for you to connect with your family, rest your feet awhile, and breathe a sigh of relief. *This* is the foundation for a charming home.

Let's start with your main living area. If your furniture is lined up along the walls around the room, with seating so far apart that you have to crank your head and pull out binoculars to see the people sitting on the sofa, your room won't look or feel comfortable. Your neck will always have a cramp. You'll be annoyed at all the shouting and the lack of eye contact. You may even start to feel antisocial or at least socially awkward! But with one simple change, your room can have the cozy ambience that nurtures a warm and welcoming conversation. Ready to try it?

Pull the seating pieces away from the walls and closer together so space between them is more inviting. Arrange comfortable chairs near the sofa, ideally in a *U* shape, so you can face the people you are talking to and have a friendly chat with them without projecting your voice across the room.

Sofas are great for two people who turn their bodies to face each other, but you will need the chairs in order to have a comfortable group conversation. If you don't have living-room chairs, borrow a couple of chairs from your dining room. Move things around until you feel more at home!

Many of us think we have to own the perfect furniture in order to begin improving our spaces, but really we just need to start with what we have, what we can find, or what we can afford right now. Don't blow your budget on dozens of accessories. Save up for the conversation areas and add to them as you are able. Be content and creative with what you have!

Next step. Make sure each chair and sofa is within reach of a place to set drinks and reading material. You should be able to reach the coffee table and end tables without standing up and walking away from the conversation area.

If you don't have a coffee table, do you have a trunk or a couple of short stools or an ottoman? Small benches, nesting tables, or stools are great flexible pieces that can be pulled into the conversation area for more seating or surfaces during a party. Don't worry about finding tables that match—an eclectic feel is much more interesting.

I actually keep quite a few extra stools and benches on hand (tucked away against a wall or under a console table) so we always have enough seating for guests, places to prop up tired feet, and tables for beverages. Short people (like me) will especially appreciate the extra footstools so our little legs can land somewhere with dignity rather than swinging around awkwardly as if we were fidgety preschoolers!

If you have comfortable seating, a coffee table and end tables for drinks, and convenient places for your feet, your conversation area will have a great foundation for comfort and you'll be ready to add more layers of ambience!

Shine a Little Light on It

You can have a room full of character with a cozy conversation area, but if the lighting is wrong, its atmosphere will never seem right. A room radiating ambience will be bathed in soft light. One glaring ceiling light (or heaven forbid, the dreaded fluorescent light) will not do a room or your pretty face any favors. Light from multiple sources will soften dark corners and warm up the room. Natural light is wonderful if you have it, and if you are planning a remodel, be sure to add lots of big windows. But even with a lot of windows, ambient lighting will elevate the mood of a home in the evenings or on dark winter days.

If you aren't yet a collector of lamps, try to become one. Trust me. Lamps will be your friends. If you are starting from scratch, you can find great, affordable lamps at garage sales and thrift stores. Look for lamps that are larger than you might normally have considered, and give yourself permission to enjoy a new shape or personality for your lamps!

Every room needs at least two large lamps near the conversation areas. Some of my rooms have three or four lamps. It's a bit of an addiction, but it's a good one because it creates the ambience I love. It's fun

Style Notes

Different lightbulbs set different moods. For lamps, I prefer bulbs that are labeled "warm light" rather than "daylight." Daylight bulbs are great where we need a lot of light, such as in a garage, but in most spaces I prefer a warm glow, so I make choices with that priority in mind. Always serve your priorities and purpose for your home.

to add in a smaller lamp or two on a console table to provide extra light and charm. Floor lamps can be a great addition too. I prefer small-scale, pharmacy-style metal lamps because they don't take up as much room as floor lamps and still add great light and personality.

A pair of lamps will make a room feel more cohesive and the design more intentional. If you can't get a set of matching lamps, bring out the spray paint and maybe invest in a set of matching lampshades. Paint and lampshades can fool the eye and do the trick. If you really want to go all out, make your own lamps! It's pretty easy and can be so fun. You can make a lamp out of just about anything. I have a couple of tutorials at The Inspired Room. Grab a cup of coffee and take a peek at them some afternoon for inspiration (or for the pure amusement of seeing me try a DIY project!).

While you're gathering inspiration, take a look at this list and consider how you can add some light to your home and life.

- *Entryway light.* I'm a big believer in having lamps for mood lighting right inside the front door. If your entry space is small, you still have some options with a wall lamp, sconce, or a small lamp on a nearby table. Even a small-scale, pharmacy-style floor lamp near a chair will do the trick. When you turn it on at night, the entry to your home will be warm, cozy, and inviting!

- *Kitchen light.* I love the unexpected presence and comfort of lamps in the kitchen. They can make a huge difference in the mood! In our castle we had a lamp right on the counter. In our current house, we don't have room on the counter, but we installed charming sconces on either side of our sink and have a lamp on the far side of the kitchen. Once the sun starts to go down, we start turning on the lamps. This comforting nighttime ritual makes our house cozy.

- *Bedroom light.* I believe having lamps on each side of the bed is a must for a shared room. Whether you use lamps on nightstands or hang two plug-in style wall sconces, good lighting invites you to read or relax. Overhead lights just won't cut it when you want to create a romantic or soothing ambience in the evenings. Select lamps that add character and personality.

- *Anywhere.* Dimmer switches are a great way to transform the mood of any room or space. If you can install a dimmer switch, you can create the right ambience day or night, depending on your whims!

The Thrill of the Hunt

Over the years, we became accustomed to using what we had or what we found on excursions to secondhand stores. Money was always tight, and expensive furniture wasn't in the budget. But even when what we had wasn't what we wished for, secondhand items allowed us to transform our house into a charming home.

I don't mind that we've lived with secondhand stuff most of our married life. In fact, I grew to love hunting and gathering unique things for our home. My husband and I have had great fun stopping in at garage sales and bringing home bargain-but-quality treasures, many of which we still have. We aren't serious antique collectors, nor are we skilled DIYers. We just have fun creating a home that has the character we love.

Our current house is half the size our castle was. I swore off flea-market shopping for a couple years because I needed to downsize and get rid of things, not add more. To love what you have, you have to be able to see it, and sometimes that means letting go of a lot of it. More recently I rounded a corner—I've eliminated what wasn't working, and I've resumed my quest to add back in only what I need. I am so happy

I made room for furnishings I will love and really use.

We have a local flea market around the corner from our church building, and many Sunday afternoons you'll find us rummaging around for something that catches our eye. The one-of-a-kind things we collect add personality to our home. Brand-new items can be just as fun, but a nice mix of old and new brings more character.

Classics may be popular for a time and then less so when the masses move on to the next trendy item, but they are always in style. I always snatch up pretty white dishes, and I add to my blue-and-white collection of teacups, plates, and jars. I love finding real brass and silver candlesticks and accessories. I collect pretty hardback books and use them all over my house as decorations (and obviously for reading material too!). Antique mirrors and interesting frames are great finds as well.

Secondhand dressers are among my favorite functional finds. I look for solid wood construction (even if they are painted) and dovetailed drawers. They are hardworking, flexible pieces that can be placed in any room. I used to collect chairs that needed new upholstery or slipcovers, but then I made peace with two facts—I didn't want to hoard furniture I was waiting to repaint, and I didn't like the hassle or the expense of reupholstering. I decided to stick to secondhand furniture that is in already good condition or find affordable new chairs (which is getting easier thanks to some of the retail chains).

Whether you select items my way or you are a go-getter with painting, reupholstering, or making slipcovers, you can transform and fall in love with your home one charming detail at a time. Don't ever feel rushed. Consider adopting my new motto: If I can't think of a way to use the item right away, it doesn't get to come home with me. Enjoy the process of adding character to your house and beauty to your life.

Start with the Right Shell

So what happens when we have arranged the furniture, added the lighting, and included accessories we love…but we still don't sense the charm and character we want for our home? No, that doesn't necessarily mean it's time to look for a new house! Perhaps the shell of the room simply needs attention. Improving the bones of the room might feel daunting, but in the long run, you'll be glad you made the effort. And happily, you can do many things *right where you are* to transform the shell of the house you already have.

The right wall color can dramatically change the feel of a home. After all, your wall color will likely cover the largest visible surface of your room. You can set the right mood and tie everything together by choosing a color that appears in fabric you already have in the room or that complements your wood furniture. To keep the color scheme from feeling too matchy, select a slightly grayed tone to soften the look.

Painting isn't the only way to create a beautiful room. To really see the shell of a room, remove all the furniture and study what you like and don't like about the space itself. I did this with our gathering room and our dining room. As soon as I removed the furniture, I could see that the room was actually fine—it was the carpet I really didn't like. To stay in my budget, I bought a couple of inexpensive area rugs to distract me from the ugly carpet.

Finally, after waiting for years, I was able to get new hardwood floors in several rooms of our home. Even though this choice meant we had to wait even longer to invest in furniture, the floors alone made the room look (and smell) so much better.

After my wood floors were installed in my living room and dining room, I was ready to do some remodeling on my kitchen. I had missed my castle kitchen so much following our move. But in those

---

Style Notes

If you are ready to make some more permanent improvements or practice your DIY skills to add to the shell of your space, you might consider adding finishing architectural details, such as chunkier window trim, wainscoting or wood-planked walls, built-ins, or tile or hardwood flooring.

earlier years in the new house, I made the best of the kitchen we had. I removed cupboard doors to add a little more personality with open shelves, and I bought an indoor–outdoor kitchen rug in a fun stripe to give my kitchen more personality. But when the time came and I could do a more significant makeover, I was ecstatic.

Without completely gutting the room or starting over, we improved some of the architectural elements so it would feel more like home. We remodeled with affordable details that brought architectural charm to strategic places without the custom-kitchen price tag. We added stock subway tile, wood-planked walls over the drywall, and attractive lighting to replace the standard builder-variety lights.

I really wanted an old island to add more texture and character to our kitchen, but instead, I beat up an unfinished piece of furniture to look old. My daughter Courtney and I took a bag of screws and nails and pounded the top of the island until it was distressed and looked like an antique. We then painted the bottom half white and stained the top a nice rich wood tone to bring out the grain. We finished off the piece with some old-looking iron hooks and some funky animal pulls on the drawers. It was fun to create a faux antique.

Even when the kitchen is a hot mess, it still feels beautiful to me. That's the benefit of loving the shell of a room—the furniture and accessories become the icing on the cake, and whatever you add makes a bigger statement.

But if you aren't yet able to do exactly what you love in your home, take heart. There are plenty of ways to find contentment with what you have.

The Art of Concealment

Some of my decorating ideas will surely shock anyone with money to burn. However, my methods won't surprise you if you face the same issues I do—limited time and money. (Ahem.) If we had a lot of both, we could do whatever we wanted. But to make things pretty when you have limitations, you have to think outside the box. I think of these limitations as opportunities to practice what I call "creative concealment."

What exactly is creative concealment, you ask? Creative conceal-ment is hiding the ugly, transforming the unlovely, and distracting from the hideous with more creativity than cash. In other words, it's adding charm and character on a budget. It buys you time to get things done.

We used creative concealment in each of our houses, but the castle took our desperation (er…that is, our inspiration) to a whole new level. Old houses have always stolen my heart, but owning one isn't always as romantic as it sounds. When you move in to an older house, you're likely to have visions of restoring it to beauty. But in reality, in the early years your money might go to not-so-pretty things, such as new sewer lines, replacements for rotted overhangs, removal of lead paint and asbestos, and new electrical panels. We became skilled in the art of averting our eyes from things we didn't really want anyone to look at. When done right, creative concealment isn't deception—it's artistry. That's what we like to think, anyway.

I'm pretty sure no one pins favorite sewer pipes to their dream-house board on Pinterest. Ah, yes. But whether your house is old or new, there is always hope when you know you can make things prettier with creative concealment even when budgets are tight.

We continue to turn to creative concealment principles in our cur-rent, much-newer house. We hide less-than-spectacular views out our back windows and deck all the time! If you follow my blog, you've seen us putting up trellises and growing wisteria in pots so we could sit out on our deck sunbathing all summer if we really wanted to. We created our own secluded, summer oasis by training vines onto trellises we bought at home-improvement stores.

Remodeling or refurnishing a house with lots of cash would be a dream, but a simple solution is often best (even if you can afford more). Being content with what you have doesn't mean things have to stay as they are. Creative concealment will give you the joy of being content because you can always make what you have *better than it was* with your creative thinking cap on.

Creative Concealments

- Curtains—homemade or stock—can transform windows that are the wrong shape or size or just plain ugly.

- Plants or baskets can hide wall outlets or cords.

- Pretty sheets or fabric panels can enclose basement laundry areas or create makeshift closets.

- Creative furniture placement can visually reshape odd rooms or disguise other issues.

- Charming shutters, blinds, or stained glass can conceal less-than-lovely views.

- Paint or stain refreshes unsightly furniture and unites mismatched pieces.

- Slipcovers renew upholstery.

- Wall hangings hide wall imperfections.

- Set pretty runners on tables to freshen their appearance.

- Mirrors hung or leaned create the illusion of more space and reflect more light in small areas.

- Throw pillows and blankets liven up old sofas.

- Planked walls add old-house character to plain drywall.

- Painted faux board-and-batten or tin ceiling tiles add nonpermanent architectural detail.

- Use craft or white paper, sheet music, book pages, or wallpaper to cover books with torn spines.

- Old doors or a curtain hung behind a bed can give the illusion of a headboard.

- Unique hardware updates boring cabinet doors.

Get Creative

Think of a home or restaurant or a sweet bed-and-breakfast you consider full of charm. *What are two of its decor elements that you could put your own spin on in your home? Try it!*

Look around your house. What feature you are tired of looking at? *How could you improve the space with a little creative concealment or a clever trick to avert the eye?*

What is unique about you and your life? *Your one-of-a-kind perspective can be a great source of inspiration and creativity.*

CHAPTER 10

Love What You Have (Even When You Don't Like It)

Home is where one starts from.
T.S. ELIOT

Most of us don't live in perfect houses. We live with furniture handed down or collected over time. We likely live in a less-than-ideal-for-us rental or a home that was not custom built to perfectly suit our taste and needs.

We might imagine it would be *so much easier* to feel the love for a house designed according to our every whim, want, and need, but creating a home is always about embracing what you have and who you are. That's where we all start.

If you have the funds, opportunity, and desire to create a perfect dream house…what a gift! That's where you start. If you need to interpret the term "dream house" with a little more flexibility, that's where you begin. You define the dream that makes sense for you right now.

I knew when we moved into the house we have now that it would never be as romantic to me as an old house, and it certainly wasn't as perfect as a custom-built house. But I also knew it was the right choice for us for the season we were in. Romance wasn't at the top of our list at this stage, and perfection never has been. In an unlikely turn of events, we became all about practicality in house hunting this time around.

Yet if I've learned any-thing at all about life thus far, it's that romance is something we can create. True love can be right in front of us even if we are certain we are currently living in the wrong house, in the wrong state, with the wrong furniture, and with the wrong budget.

Real-life romance is much sweeter and more precious because it is built on *what you actually have*. This home is yours to nurture and cherish in whatever ways you can right now. Even if you won't live here forever, you can make the best of the time you have in this house. You can live life to the full while you are here.

You can embrace sentimental memories you've gathered along the way, make things a little fancier, and embellish them to be more to your liking. Your home can evolve over time, and you can give it little creative touches to make it better than it was, even if it can't be perfect in this season of life. That is often my goal with a project—just to make it better than it was.

It's worth investing the energy to take care of the house you have. Eventually you'll feel that love come back to you. No other family or life or home is exactly like yours, so celebrate the gift of what you have within your four walls.

To be authentic in your style, your home should be a true reflection of your family, heart, and life rather than a duplication of what you see online or in a magazine. Those are sources of inspiration, of course, but to create an authentic home is to embrace the personality, quirks, limitations, and uniqueness of what you have to work with.

Finding contentment wherever we are, right there in the middle of all those imperfections, annoying frustrations, and glaring projects piling up around us, is how we begin to nurture a love for our home. The truth is, new furniture or a better house will never really satisfy—they will just set new, higher standards for what is acceptable to us for our comfort and contentment. When you take care of what you have and find joy right where you are, you set the right tone and expectations for contentment in all circumstances moving forward. Whether things get better or worse, our standard will be to love what we have and be grateful for it (even when we might not like it).

We can let ourselves get stuck in a rut of "woe is me" thinking, or we can dwell in the art of creative possibility. Accept what you have as blessings and opportunities, and you will discover a surprising sense of contentment.

Use What You Can Find

Embracing flexibility when making design decisions for our home allows us to see that there is more than one way to accomplish our goals. Once I was determined to find a new buffet for my small and informal dining room. We have a rickety hand-me-down dining table, a charming but too-small rolling wood-and-metal cart, and an assortment of chairs.

I dreamed of a big, charming farm table and chairs, but all I really wanted at that moment was to replace the rolling cart (which was too short for the wall) with a long, shallow buffet with storage for a few entertaining pieces. I had a picture in my mind of exactly what I wanted. I had some money set aside, so I started the search. I searched high. I searched low. Nothing. Everything I wanted was too expensive or not right.

One day while shopping, I stumbled upon a small, rustic wood cabinet. It wasn't what I was looking for, but I realized it would fit nicely in an unused corner of the dining room. So it came home with me to hold glasses and napkin holders. Now that I was open to more creative options, I was inspired to look around my own house to see what other solutions I might come up with. (Our homes can be the best places to shop because we look at what we already have in a new light.)

As I was meandering through the entry to the kitchen on my way to my morning coffee, I happened to notice that my flea-market dresser was just 20 steps from the dining room. Silly me. That underused dresser could be cleared out and used for the napkins and placemats I wanted to store in a new dining-room buffet. It's a wonder I thought of that even before my coffee, but then again, what took me so long to think of it in the first place?

WE TRULY *treasure* AN *object of beauty* WHEN WE MAKE IT *a part* OF *our life* RATHER THAN KEEPING IT *apart* FROM *our life*

Sometimes I just shake my head at myself for being so slow to recognize solutions that are right under my own nose. I didn't even have to move the dresser—it was perfectly acceptable right where it was. Storage needs were solved.

Soon after this discovery of the obvious, I found two great chairs for my dining room at a deal I couldn't pass up. Had I bought a brand-new buffet, I wouldn't have had room (or the budget) for the new chairs. I was able to rearrange seating in the dining room to accommodate the new chairs at the ends of the table. Two rattan chairs I previously had at the table now sit on either side of that smallish rolling cart, finishing off the wall nicely.

The too-small rolling cart is now perfectly sized on the wall (roll eyes at self). My dining room now feels more complete, I have plenty of storage for entertaining, and I have ample chairs for guests too! Sometimes a good or even great solution is right in front of us—we just have to open our eyes and be flexible.

Use What You Love

The moment I was given my antique glass European sugar shaker, I fell in love with its unique charm. But I was also struck with fear of its impending doom. I just knew we would break it—if not that day, then surely within a month. We are clumsy like that. But I loved it so much I resisted the urge to hide it safely in a cupboard. I set it on our kitchen counter so we could use and appreciate it. And we did!

Turns out, that antique wasn't delicate at all. It survived many uses and all of our family moves. That one piece added incredible charm and character to our daily experience.

Eighteen years after I feared its demise, it cracked from the wear and tear of twisting the lid and refilling it so many times. We truly treasure an object of beauty when we make it a part of our life rather than keeping it apart from our life.

Isn't that the great temptation—to play it safe? We don't bring home or use what we really love out of fear of the what-ifs. What if we ruin something we prize? What if our favorite fabric fades or a beautiful wool rug gets worn?

Yes, those pretty dishes might break someday. But why live with ugly plastic dishes you don't love simply because they are supposedly indestructible? Do we really want to choose long-lasting ugliness over something we love? I love living with what is useful *and* beautiful. Using the things we love and having them on display adds layers of character to our home and happiness to our day.

Do you not have pretty everyday dishes? Well, you need them! You really do! Why drink out of an ugly cup when you can sip coffee or tea out of an elegant or clever one? Attractive doesn't necessarily mean expensive. Don't fall for that. Start shopping at resale, thrift, and discount home stores for your basic necessities, such as cups and bowls in attractive shapes and colors. Your dishes don't even have to match—just be sure they are pretty to you.

I even treat myself now and then to a fancy new coffee mug from the discounted sale section of more expensive stores because they often don't cost any more than the cheap stuff. The only downside I've found to having pretty dishes is that I struggle to decide which mug to use when I pour my morning coffee. Decisions, decisions! But that's also the best part.

I implore you to start gradually replacing ugly everyday necessities with things you love. You'll thank me every time you pull a lovely cereal bowl out for breakfast. I'd much rather have stacks of pretty plates we use every day than a useless *objet d'art* sitting on a shelf. I love to collect mismatched inexpensive white dishes too. I never worry about breaking dishes because we have such a fun assortment, we can easily find a replacement to mix in.

Isn't the point to make your home well-loved and full of signs of life? Life is far too short to live with ugly things or worry about a little scuff mark here and there. Smiles will eventually cause wrinkles, but that doesn't mean we should stop smiling! Live with things you love, things that make you happy.

Mix It Up

Creating a home you love is an experiment of mixing and matching to find your own unique style. You don't have to resort to the security of a preselected furniture collection or a bedding set with all matching pillows and comforter. A unique style really isn't difficult to create. Be brave and fearless enough to try something you haven't seen before or to put things together in a fresh new way without overthinking it. You can pair old with new, traditional with cottage, painted with wood. You can even mix wood tones. Most of us need to start with furniture we have already acquired one way or another. Perhaps we inherited someone else's furniture or we have various pieces representing different times of life and assorted trends. If you are frustrated by your current selection, I guarantee you that mixing and matching will make your style unique and interesting. You don't have to love everything individually to love the room.

Mixing up what you have becomes a fun game. If your furniture is dark or traditional and you want a lighter, cottage vibe or more modern look, there are creative and clever ways to update your style without painting everything or tossing your furniture to the curb.

If you have some quality or classic pieces, I say *keep*, *use*, and *enjoy* them! Paint them. Refinish them. Slipcover them. Try them in another room. Or pair them up with accessories, like throw blankets or pillows, to give them a new look. If you just can't find a way to use what you have, let someone else have the fun of trying the pieces in their home.

Our smallish master bedroom is the poster child for mixing and matching and using what is available. In this one space, I have a dark wood traditional sleigh bed; a wood armoire from my mom; a modern, painted, gold dresser; a gray-blue console table as a nightstand; a taupe settee that once graced our living room; a black, painted bookcase; and a black, antique chinoiserie cabinet my grandparents brought home from Thailand many years ago.

It's quite a blend of furniture, don't you think? It's also a true reflection of our life right now. We didn't paint or refinish anything or deliberately put them all together in the room for any particular reason outside of practicality. However, a little mixing and matching helped to make it all look complete and intentional. I tied everything together with a fresh coat of soothing gray-toned paint on the walls and a mix of art and accessories, including a modern, metallic, round mirror over the headboard. I finished the room's look with an assortment of bedding.

The result of the mix-match approach to our bedroom decor? It's one big happy family of random furniture that reflects our taste and our ever-evolving home story.

-Style Notes-

If you have a traditional bedroom set with matching night-stands and dresser, you can get a less formal look by putting the nightstands in another bedroom to mix up the set. Or paint the nightstands in a lighter shade or the dresser in a cheery color to brighten the mood. Add a fun rug, and you'll have a brand-new look. Changing one feature of a furniture piece can give it a new home in any room. You don't even need paint. You can embellish bookcases or cabinets with heavy-duty wrapping paper, wallpaper, or maps. Look for textures and designs you love and make them a part of what you have.

Calling my style eclectic is freeing because it validates everything I want or need to include in a room. Is that ridiculous? Go ahead and say it. I'm okay with that. Eclectic and ridiculous reflect who I am. And that means my style is perfect for me.

Honestly, when you're mixing and matching, some combinations won't look great together at first glance or maybe even second glance, but you can make just about anything work with a little creative ingenuity.

The more you use this method to love what you have, the easier it is to evolve your style over time. An eclectic house isn't as easily dated because it can continually evolve with you.

Put It on Repeat

Repetition is an easy way to use random pieces you have collected over time and unify them into a cohesive look for your home. Take a quick scan of the room you are working on. What do you see too much of right now? Is there a lot of competing color or pattern? An abundance of painted pieces? A lot of wood?

The repetition of a neutral in a room will let the color pop and help to unify the room. Solids can balance out patterns and give your eye a little rest. The addition of natural wood tones can break up an abundance of painted or upholstered pieces, and conversely, you can break up a lot of wood with fabric-covered or painted pieces.

The repetition of white on walls, woodwork, slipcovers, painted tables, or accessories can simplify all the random patterns and collections you have as well as brighten up your space. Your eye will find rest in the consistency of a color palette even if you have many mismatched items in the room.

You can also unify your home with a color you love. Our fairy-tale cottage felt like a hodgepodge of things until we added a lot of green with fabric, paint, and accessories. The more we brought in that color, the more intentional our hodgepodge of furnishings looked!

Green might not be your thing, so choose whatever color you like and use it throughout the house in your choice of furniture, accessories, or paint. I love a house that has a nice color flow. We've tried this same trick in our current house with a lot of white and shades of grays and blues. It took a few years to repaint all our walls, but the results were worth the effort. The repetition of color tones really does work to bring harmony to a space. Aim to use a color at least three times in a room.

Repetition can also be accomplished when you use multiples of certain pieces, such as several throw pillows in matching fabric or several frames painted all the same color. Your eye will follow the repeated elements, and your style will feel more cohesive and welcoming.

Go Bigger and Bolder

We've all been there. You're out shopping, and you want to buy something new for your home. You really don't know what you want or need, but you fully intend to come home with something fun to make your home more personal. You deserve it. It's your mission for the day. So you wander through some shops, looking for the missing ingredient to add to your living room or your office. It's fun to consider all the options, and you're certain you'll find exactly what you want if you look in enough places.

Blogger *Home* ♥ *Love* Story

Creating a Place to Gather

We bought our 1970s Oregon home as a fixer-upper ten years ago, and we slowly remodeled as we could. Making it perfect was never the goal. Early on, my husband and I decided that no matter what our surroundings, the benefit of owning a home was to share it with others through the conduits of love and food. We hosted dinner party after dinner party with a tiny kitchen, original bathrooms, and funky lighting throughout the house.

We started upgrading by creating functional spaces to welcome people into. Outside we planted 14 raised beds, providing many garden-to-table meals. Eventually we tore down a couple of kitchen walls and built a giant center island that has become the hub of the home, where guests hang out and we can cook together as a family. With gratitude, every decision we make supports our motto: Home is a place where people gather, where they feel safe, inspired, nurtured, and loved, and where they are fed.

—Sandy Coughlin,
of the blog The Reluctant Entertainer

Then your eyes find *it*. That adorable little accessory you want and can afford (bonus!). Perhaps, for the sake of this illustration, you found a small ceramic bunny…or bird or whatever trend you are convinced will transform your room from blah to wow. Maybe not a big wow but at least a little *nice touch*. The sales clerk wraps it up nicely, and you smile all the way home. You quickly unwrap that sweet bunny as you come in the front door and begin rushing from end table to bookshelf, looking for its proper home. Here? No. Over there? Ugh. No. FOR THE LOVE. WHY?

Then reality hits. It was so precious in the store, but in the spaciousness of your rooms, you don't even notice it. You are deflated. The sad truth is, the tiny bunny doesn't make a statement. At all.

You are distraught but determined. You drag out a dozen more accessories, trying to make the statement you want, piling things up all around that little bunny until you can barely see his wee eyes peering out from the rubble. Two hours later your room looks worse than when you started. Eventually the bunny ends up covered with dust in a closet, and you repeat the process again a few months later with a tiny owl. Right? I know. It's okay. We've all been there.

How do these well-meaning shopping trips go so wrong? The intention was good. You want to live with what you love. I mean, who can find fault with a bunny? But such shopping trips often end in frustration because we expect too much from little accessories. They won't make the dramatic impact we hope for.

When it comes to loving your home, bigger and bolder accessories will make a much stronger impact in your room. Tiny accessories might make you happy, but don't expect them to transform a space. They help tell your story but in a more subtle way. Give them a small corner or shelf where they can nestle in.

When you want to make a big splash in a room, target key focal points of your home and go for accessories that are bolder than you think you need. Try putting a giant pair of candlesticks on a coffee table, a large vase on a mantel, or an oversized lantern in your dining room. You'll really notice the difference in the room. Go bigger and bolder with accessories to add eye-catching personality to your home.

Love What You See

Even things we love—such as our mementos, collections, favorite colors, patterned fabrics, accessories, and furnishings—can create a bit of chaos in the house. Once you add in the understandable signs of life around the house, sometimes all you can see is clutter.

If you walk into a room and every wall or surface has something loud to say, you can feel overwhelmed just trying to figure out where to look or what to listen to! In fact, the effect might send you off to run and hide. It's like going to a party full of extroverts when you're an introvert. (*Heh heh heh.*)

I love a house that comes to life through fun visual interest—contrasts in color, playful patterns, creative accessories, meaningful artwork. Those things make me happy! My home is a lively yet relaxed and informal place, filled with memories and things we love. Yet for my

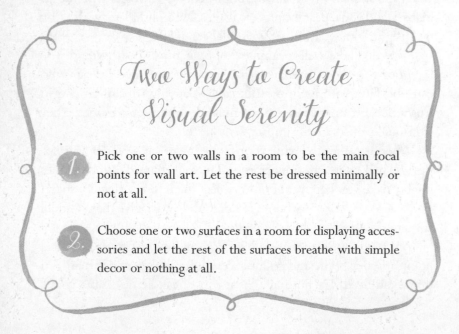

Two Ways to Create Visual Serenity

1. Pick one or two walls in a room to be the main focal points for wall art. Let the rest be dressed minimally or not at all.

2. Choose one or two surfaces in a room for displaying accessories and let the rest of the surfaces breathe with simple decor or nothing at all.

sanity, I want my decor to be somewhat thoughtful and ordered so the house doesn't overwhelm me with too many busy or random vignettes and accessories.

If you have too many things on display or scattered throughout the house without a forethought to showcase them, you will feel the same disorder and unsettledness you feel with clutter. It's just too much. Fortunately a few organizational tricks can bring a sense of calm order to our decor so we can love what we see.

Did you know that accessories have a greater impact when there are fewer of them competing for attention? Your accessories need room to breathe. And likewise, collections will have more significance when they are displayed together than when they are scattered. Not every surface needs a vignette, and not every vignette needs a lot of accessories to make a statement. You can create a more effective and design-friendly impact with fewer tchotchkes!

If you love collecting accessories, paring down might be challenging because you can't bear to part with them. I suggest going on a rotation diet with your accessories. Pick a few favorites for the season and let them have a place of honor. Put the rest away. In the next season, let another collection be in the limelight. You'll likely appreciate your mementos even more because your home will be an ever-changing canvas.

Deliberate and careful color and pattern choices can also contribute to the serenity of your room. I feel more visual serenity in my home when I can step back, look across to rooms within my sight, and feel as if everything is playing together nicely without too many things competing or calling out for attention. That's why I stick to mostly neutral backdrops of soft wall colors that connect visually from room to room. I use liberal doses of white or neutral throughout my home to let my accessories and patterns shine rather than compete.

Not to say I don't want pops of color, fun patterns, or unique pieces here and there! I have plenty of those in my home. I love adding whimsical fabrics and seasonal colors. When a home has a general sense of visual serenity, there is always an opportunity to go a little crazy and let some elements steal the show because other areas will just sit back, quietly adding to the ambience. Everything in a room shouldn't command the same amount of attention.

Of course, what feels overwhelming or loud to me may feel inspiring to someone else, and vice versa. If it feels right to you and you love it, then it's right for your home and you should embrace it. The important thing is that you love what you see as you walk through your home.

Give yourself time to turn your house into a home you love. Always remember to start a project by taking some before pictures so you can celebrate each accomplishment and little transformation.

Love It

What is holding you back from loving what you have?

What things do you have in your house that you should love, except you don't? *Paint is your friend. You can transform and unify frames, candlesticks, accessories, furniture, baskets, stools, trays, hardback books, lamps, chairs, tables, and decorative plates. If you don't like it, you can change it with paint. What are you waiting for? Go find something you tolerate and transform it into something you love.*

What accessories might refresh a room and boost your spirits? *Bring in pieces that inspire you and make you enjoy spending time in your home.*

CHAPTER 11

Creating a Haven

Ah! there is nothing like staying at home for real comfort.
JANE AUSTEN

Remember your dream house from the end of chapter 1? It's time to start creating a meaningful life there.

Your home should be your haven. It should be a place where you feel welcomed. It's your safe place in the world to create memories and live out dreams. It's where you raise your family, love your spouse, and find the security and confidence to set out on a journey to achieve your goals. Your home is a place to rejuvenate your sagging spirit, relax your weary mind, and recharge your worn-down creativity. It's a place to welcome friends and an oasis where you can shut out the world.

The home you have can be everything you want it to be—simply take the steps to make it happen. Our realities won't always reflect the dream vision. But guess what? That's okay. Creating a comfortable haven is about bringing our dreams in line with the craziness of our reality to create something meaningful and true—a beautiful home with a heartbeat that inspires our life.

A Place That Welcomes

A welcoming home is more than a place to greet a neighbor who might knock at your front door. It's a safe haven for your family. Paying attention to the small details can help you care for the ones who live there and the guests you invite inside.

Your initial opportunity to express warmth happens in your entry area. This first impression says something about your personality whether you intend it to or not! You can create a space that is as lively, laid-back, fun, or charming as you.

Our dogs, Jack and Lily, help set the tone for our entry. You can't come in our door without Jack flinging himself in the air with an ungraceful, lunging action and Lily attempting with all her might to give you a big kiss on your face. Even if you don't have such an excitable welcoming committee, your entry will embrace all who cross your threshold (including you) one way or another.

Now let's just pause for a moment and quietly address what might be the unpardonable homemaker sin. If you have a Christmas wreath on the front door and it's December, you are off the hot seat. In fact, you are homemaker of the year right there, so give yourself a high five. But if the Christmas wreath is up and it is May (nervous laugh)…my, oh my, how time flies! After dark tonight would be a great time to sneak that crunchy evidence into the recycling bin and destroy the evidence. Trust me. I get it. I once had a petrified pumpkin on my porch until spring. I won't cast the first stone if you'll forgive me for the pumpkins. There—our darkest secrets are out of the way. Moving on…

Let's look at six ways to make the entrance to your dream home a gracious, welcoming place.

- *Keep your entry tidy and personable.* Maintain an inviting space that is uncluttered and still embellished with small, personal touches that tell the story of your family and set the stage for an authentic home.

- *Light it well inside and out.* A porch light and an entry light are two essentials for a welcoming home. If you don't have room for a lamp in your entry, find a clip-on light to illuminate a painting and to add a dash of sparkle.

- *Express your family's personality with art and accessories.* Add something unexpected and even a little whimsical to invite guests into your family's story. What better place for a fun conversation starter?

- *Pay attention to details.* Does your door have fresh paint? Are your house numbers visible outside? When was the last time you replaced your doormat?

- *Use the space you have.* It doesn't matter whether you have a formal entry, or you walk straight into a living room, or you have a side entrance that everyone prefers. You can add a few entry-like details to any of these spaces. Here's a starter list: a floating shelf for keys, a colorful rug, and a mirror to check for spinach in your teeth when you answer the door or head out for a busy day.

- *Make room for daily life.* Do you have places for shoes, coats, backpacks, dog leashes, and mail? Everything that comes into your entry needs to have a designated landing spot, or it will end up in a pile right at your front door. It's hard to feel welcome when you open the door and immediately trip on smelly gym bags. Am I right?

We have only one small closet on our main floor, so I let our real-life necessities, such as coats and shoes, become a part of the charm of our entry by providing space for them on wall hooks and in baskets.

We use hooks for more than just coats. We hang up cute canvas bags to organize items for errands and for longer trips. We keep track of umbrellas, dog leashes, backpacks, and purses and keep them away from inquisitive pups. Always have enough hooks to provide plenty of space for guests to hang their coats to save them from having to dig around in a dark coat closet after a gathering.

Let your entry be a happy first impression and inspiration for the life you live at home and the way you want to connect with others. If your entryway looks tired, worn, or cluttered, or if it doesn't set the right tone for your home, you might want to set aside some time this week to give it a little extra love.

A Place That Is Warm

My family has always had fun creating a special atmosphere in which to greet guests. We aren't the formal dinner-party type, but we love fashioning a casually festive ambience for simple gatherings with special touches. We line our walkway to the front door with small white candles in mason jars. We turn on the outside lights, sweep off the porch, dust off the cobwebs, and polish the doorknob. We set mood lighting in the house with adjusted lamps and candles that also offer a subtle scent. We hit Play, and background music livens up the atmosphere. Then we take one last look to see what else we can do to make our home feel as cozy to guests as possible.

In our earlier years I read a book on marriage that suggested greeting your husband at the door with the same warmth you would offer to guests. Yes! I loved the idea. In theory. But as I let that sink in, it clashed with the reality of my long days home alone all by myself with many small, crying people covered in squash and Cheerios. I treasure those days, but even the memory of them can be pretty epically exhausting.

It was unlikely that at the end of a day I would manage to be relaxed and genuinely welcoming, let alone having lined the walkway with candles in preparation for Jerry's dinnertime arrival. Truth be told, my smile sometimes looked a bit more like a grimace, and I was usually ready to just hand him the babies as I ran out the door to Starbucks for a double shot of peace and quiet.

But in the pursuit of marital happiness and a warm and welcoming haven for our family, I realized there was a simple way to set a new tone for our home. Besides brushing my teeth and wiping the baby snot off my shoulders, I could walk over to the front door at dusk and turn on the outside lights and at least one inside lamp. That I could do.

Turning on the lamps was a little signal to Jerry that I was happy he was coming home. It was a reminder to me of the mood I could create for our home with a few intentional daily rituals. At that pivotal hour of our mutually long day, the atmosphere of our home offered the escape we both craved. That simple ritual was my way of saying, "Welcome home, I'm glad you're here (and not just because I've been plotting my escape to Starbucks)."

Don't we all want to feel that way when we enter our home? Welcomed warmly? Hospitality toward guests is important. Creating a place to extend warm welcomes to our family should be a priority too.

You know how a dog wants to run over to greet you with a big, sloppy but happy kiss when you walk in the door? The greeting makes you feel loved (and maybe even slightly overwhelmed by his enthusiasm). My son always gives me a sweet little wave when I drop him off at school—a tradition that still means the world to me now that he's a teen. In turn, it means a lot to him if I have a snack ready for him when he arrives home (boys are always starving).

Perhaps your family could adopt some special homecoming and departure routines to establish that same warm, loving atmosphere when people arrive home or head out for the day. Here are ten ideas you might want to incorporate into your family's traditions.

- Greet family with a kiss, a smile, and a hug.

- Light a candle and turn on your lamps for a cozy, welcoming ambience as you and your family come in the door.

- Have a drink or snack ready for after-school (or after-work!) enjoyment. It's wonderful to know you have something ready in the fridge or pantry to set out while dinner gets started.

- Turn on some music when you arrive home. It might set just the perfect tone for a relaxing evening.

- Allow a buffer period of time before asking questions and discussing the day's problems. My husband used to sit in the car for ten minutes to decompress from the stress of the day before walking in the door so he could enter the house ready to enjoy the evening.

- Create a stress-free departure. Nothing is as flustering (for you and your family) as trying to get out the door when you are stressed by disorganization. Make it a priority to prepare ahead of time for your departure so you can walk out the door calmly and on time instead of panicking to find your shoes and keys.

- Keep your entry tidy and welcoming so your house is one you want to come home to and hate to leave! Give everyone a hook and a basket to keep their belongings organized and off the floor.

- Always pause long enough to give a proper goodbye. When my kids would leave for their school carpool, I always made sure I was at the door to send them off with a quick hug and prayer for their day (as my mom did for me). Those memories are precious.

- Use timers to prepare for your warm welcome. Timers can be wonderful reminders to turn on a few lamps, turn on the heat on a cold night, or turn on a coffeepot or a crockpot with a hot drink, an appetizer, or dinner.

- Establish an evening ritual for meaningful conversation and reconnection. Before discussing any negatives, encourage your family to talk about the best part of their day. Keeping the welcome-home routine positive (rather than pointing out what chores weren't done or what else went wrong that day!) will transform the rest of the evening.

Establish warm welcome traditions that make coming home the sweetest part of everyone's day.

A Place of Hospitality

What characteristics of your home invite friends and family to stay awhile?

Jerry and I consider our house a haven and retreat for our family from the busy outside world, and we also feel it is important to make meaningful connections with others inside our home.

Even when we first moved into this house as renters and had hardly any furniture, we made a point to invite new friends into our home. Back then our walls were still bathed in the swine color, our carpet was an unfortunate shade of brown, and our home had no hint of our personality. But those things never stopped us from establishing connections with others.

I believe that inviting others into our homes encourages us to form deeper bonds of community. When gatherings are simple, intentional, and meaningful, the warmth and love of our homes are gifts we can offer to people we invite in. Through the offering of those gifts, you and I can more fully appreciate the blessings of friendship.

Fortunately, I love hospitality. I love creating the mood, setting the table, and preparing the atmosphere. But if the idea of a gathering at your home panics you, don't worry! Connecting with people in your home doesn't require a big formal dining room, a large food budget, or fancy party plans. It isn't about impressing people with your home or your culinary skills.

My favorite way to connect with others in our home is to host small groups around an informal theme that makes hospitality enjoyable for me and fun for guests. Girls nights are fun because we can break out the chocolate, set up the coffee bar, and curl up on sofas to chat, laugh, and cry together.

Find a style that works for you so you can open the door with confidence, invite others in, and make friends feel comfortable as you get to know each other better in the safe haven of your home. Relationship building matters so much more than having the perfect house style or budget.

Give yourself the freedom to find a style and rhythm that works for you and your family so you can experience the meaningful layer of connection that hospitality brings to your home.

A Place of Order

Do you find yourself chanting this mantra several times a day? "Serenity now, serenity now…" Yeah, I thought so. The more you have going on in life and the busier things get, the more you will crave a sense of peaceful order at home. I know I need that! Your home should be your oasis from the world (even when things get a little crazy in the house). You can't always change your outward circumstances, but you can bring a little more order to the house so it can become the calm haven you desire.

As fun as it is to make visual statements—those *ta da!* moments—it's also very important to create statements of *calm* to counter the inevitable chaos of daily life. Deep breath. Not to worry, this is something we can do without going to Target with a giant gift card in hand. Hang with me!

Reducing clutter and visual chaos is an important way to create serenity at home. When your home is filled with stuff—be it random junk you don't need, piles of papers, dirty dishes, unfinished projects, things you don't like, old mementos, or even too much good stuff, like an abundance of accessories or furnishings—you'll feel chaotic inside too.

Our souls need room to breathe. The more stuff we have littered on every surface, the more we'll feel as if we're running in circles without ever moving our feet. Nobody's got energy for that.

EVERY TIME YOU

say goodbye TO

SOMETHING

YOU DON'T NEED RIGHT NOW

YOU WILL *breathe*

A LITTLE *deeper*

Honestly, if you and I did away with about half the stuff we don't need in our houses, we would instantly feel calmer. Getting rid of the excess and creating order with what remains will bring the serenity we need to feel balanced.

First things first—you can't organize excess clutter. Plain and simple: No organization system is ever going to work if you have too much stuff. So always start any organization project by getting rid of what you don't need, have too much of, or can do without. Imagine how freeing it will be to stop shuffling the clutter!

If something no longer fits your taste or is holding you back from enjoying your home, let it go! This step isn't much fun at first, but it will be rewarding once you've done it. Every time you say goodbye to something you don't need right now, you will breathe a little deeper.

Once you have only what you really need in a room, it's time to get organized. Creating order in rooms that have limited storage will require a little creativity. One of my key organizing systems involves using lidded baskets to store things I need but don't want to see all the time. I don't suggest you use baskets to enable you to hoard more clutter, but they are wonderful storage solutions for anything that needs a designated home, and they provide visual serenity (and great texture!) to a room.

Baskets can rally remotes, video cords, game accessories, extra pantry items, seasonal dishes and decor, office supplies, and even such random items as dog leashes, spare shoes, and extra toilet paper. If you use something regularly but don't want to store it in the garage or risk losing it under the house or in the attic, it can be held in a basket in the most appropriate room. I collect baskets whenever I find a good deal. Baskets or even pretty, lidded boxes can provide serenity in every room. I often stack them in a corner, on shelves, or under footstools or console tables so they become a part of the decor.

Declutter one area at a time and then declare that space a "no more clutter" zone. It's amazing how great it feels to have even one room completely under control!

Havens for Others

Serving others is an opportunity to make a difference in some one's life and gain better perspective on your own. Here are two organizations I support that provide homes and skills for young women in need. What could be more important than helping create a haven for another?

- *Mercy House.* Mercy House exists to empower and advocate for pregnant teens, single mothers, and women in poverty all over the world through awareness, employment, and support in the name of Jesus. Learn more at mercyhousekenya.org.

- *Door to Grace.* Door to Grace provides restorative care services and safe shelter for children who are survivors of commercial sexual exploitation. Check out doortograce.org.

A Place That Rejuvenates and Inspires

What good is a haven if it doesn't provide you a place to rejuvenate your emotions, body, and spirit? Give yourself permission to enjoy peace and quiet every day. If you take care of yourself, you will be better equipped to face the day's challenges.

I've occasionally let myself get so busy I got stressed out and didn't take care of myself emotionally, physically, or spiritually. Big mistake! Having time to rejuvenate yourself is part of setting a healthy tone for your home.

Create a small corner in your home where you can think or relax for a while. Place a comfy chair there with soft lighting and a candle, and keep favorite books, a gratitude journal, or magazines at the ready. Spend a little time every morning in solitude, and you'll be much more equipped to face the day. In fact, I bet just *seeing* your quiet corner will lower your stress level. I often retreat to my own little world, where I can be alone with my thoughts, pray, and breathe in the silence away from the busyness of the rest of our home.

A rejuvenation space can be especially important to a marriage. Staying at a quaint bed-and-breakfast is romantic, but that was rarely in the budget outside of anniversaries when we were raising our young family. So it's always been important to us to create a sacred space right in our own home as a haven from the world.

OUR HOMES SHOULD *inspire us* TO GO OUT INTO THE WORLD TO DO GREAT THINGS & THEN *welcome* US BACK FOR *refreshment*

Style Notes

Look around your house right now. Do you see sweet reminders of your gifts, accomplishments, blessings, and goals? Or are you overwhelmed by evidence of past mistakes and failures? Go through your house room by room and remove whatever doesn't inspire you to be who you want to be. If something is a source of discouragement, out it goes! Better an empty room than a room that holds you back.

Fill your home with things that lift you up, make you happy, and fill you with gratitude. Your home should be a reflection of all that is good in your life so you will be inspired to follow your dreams with confidence!

We decided early on in marriage that if we had the money, we'd rather save up $200 to invest in a room we can enjoy 364 nights a year in our home than spend $200 for one night away. Not to say we didn't like to get away or take vacations, but our priority was to create a wonderful life right under our own roof.

Because we spend much of our week connecting with people online, in person, at church, and at local coffee shops and restaurants, Jerry and I crave time alone at home because that recharges our energy. We pay special attention to filling our home, and especially our bedroom, with special mementos and furnishings that create a sanctuary for both of us every day of the year.

Collections of artwork and accessories remind us of the getaways we've enjoyed through the years. We also surround ourselves with personal notes, art, quotes, and other special reminders of our romance to keep that part of our life a priority. We don't have a TV in our room, but when we did we kept it behind our armoire doors. Scented candles, soft music, clean and luxurious sheets, and a tidy room all contribute to the feeling of an escape at the end of the day.

In order to capture the true essence of a B and B, we have a lock on our door to keep family out. Mom of the year? Here is my thought on creating a getaway in our own house. You cannot have a true escape if you allow your door to be open all evening long. Even if you're just enjoying a good book alone, you deserve a place to savor peace away from the hustle and bustle of your home. I enter my room and shut the door frequently just to hear myself think.

If you do not have a lock but you do have kids, I encourage you to teach them about knocking on doors and waiting until they are invited in before entering. And even better, if you have kids old enough to read, make a sign for your door that reminds them that you are having a few moments to yourself. I know that isn't really an option when kids are tiny, but once they are grade-school age, you can expect them to respect your privacy for a short while each day. This is important for your sanity, so don't feel guilty about having your own B and B escape right in your own home!

The outside world can be a stressful place, but with a little attention to our home and the way we live in it, we really can find that sanctuary we all need. Our homes should inspire us to go out into the world to do great things, and they should welcome us back for refreshment. We give ourselves and others a gift when we create a home that inspires and even challenges us to be the people we want to be.

Get Organized

If your home lacks order, you won't feel relaxed. Is there a room in your house where you want to feel a sense of serenity? What is causing the chaos? *Remove the clutter, the excess furniture, and unnecessary accessories.*

Which items can be organized into baskets or drawers? Which pieces of furniture can be moved or removed to make the space cozier? *Consider what will make your area spacious and inviting so that you will be eager to enjoy the room.*

CHAPTER 12

Savoring the Seasons

There is a time for everything and a season
for every activity under the heavens.
ECCLESIASTES 3:1

I love the gradual evolution of the seasons. I am delighted as bit by little bit, layer by layer the seasons unfold. Just as I am growing tired of the dark, blustery days of winter, the pink buds blossom on the trees to reassure me that this season will give way to a new, brighter one. And just as I start to long for my favorite warm sweaters and boots and the freedom to turn on my oven for a pot of stew, the leaves change from green to yellow, and I feel that familiar crispness in the air. A new season begins.

Your own outdoor, seasonal experience will depend on which part of the country you live in. Embracing that same seasonal rhythm of change can help you breathe new life into your home. Seasons rejuvenate our energy level and our surroundings.

I can grow tired and complacent with too much sameness day in and day out. Perhaps you do too. My restless spirit is often in search of something different to reenergize me. Yet I also find myself longing for the familiarity of pleasant rituals and quiet graces to mark the return of each season, such as opening the window to usher in a breath of fresh, spring air or lighting a spice-scented candle on an autumn-themed table.

Each season offers us something new and something familiar for our daily routine.

Enjoy the Rhythm of Nesting

Some people are undoubtedly summer people. Some are fall or winter people. Or we might feel a little conflicted. Maybe we prefer one particular season but our home or style seems better suited to another. Perhaps your house is filled with cozy fall decor, or maybe you lean toward a coastal-inspired summer ambience. It's good to embrace your style and what inspires you!

Close your eyes for a moment and picture your dream house again. Is it spring or summer there? Fall? Winter?

I am fond of each season, so I don't want to live in just one throughout the entire year. I want my home to flow effortlessly from one season to the next because I find something to embrace in every season. I really want an all-season house. Is that too much to ask? I want my home to

SEASONS OFFER US OPPORTUNITIES ALL THROUGH THE YEAR TO refresh our home & rekindle our gratitude FOR WHAT WE HAVE

feel warm, cozy, and inviting in the winter and carefree, light, and airy in the summertime.

I'm not sure why, but that leap from one extreme to another makes me think about mullets. I know. Random. You've probably seen a mullet. The infamous bi-level haircut that was supposed to please everyone because it covered all the options—from business in the front to the party in the back.

Setting aside the unsettling question of why mullets would ever come to my mind in the first place, mullets do represent an abrupt change from one level to the next...which is *not* what I want in my home. I want my house to flow gracefully from season to season.

A mullet can't make up its mind, so it gives you whiplash as you try to understand what just happened. You know what I mean? No? Are you giving me a blank stare? Okay, before I get so far off course that you are certain I've lost my mind (I respect that), I'll regroup my thoughts.

I crave a gentler approach to nesting all through the year. I decorate my home to the relaxed ebb and flow of time. A sanctuary emerges in every season when we are intentional and take the time to create and enjoy a home we love. Seasons offer us opportunities all through the year to refresh our homes and rekindle our gratitude for what we have.

When I see evidence of a new season in my home—a wreath on the door, a candle burning in the entry, or pumpkin bread in the oven—I feel renewed energy for life and my family. I get excited about the process of seasonal nesting because each transition represents a new way to love my family, a new reason to feel blessed, and new inspiration to keep my priorities in order.

The turning of leaves in the yard, the sound of rain on the roof, and the budding of flowers in the garden reveal the slow rhythm of beautiful moments we can follow as we shape a life we adore.

Fall in Love with Autumn

Details of my affair are pretty well known around the Internet. It isn't something I've tried to hide. (Awkward silence.) You know, the love affair I have with fall! (Nervous shuffling and deep sighs of relief all around.) Fall is my favorite—I'm not ashamed to admit it!

I love the way the sun filters softly through the trees, casting beautiful, crisp shadows on the walls. The slight chill in the air is refreshing and brisk, inviting me to warm up inside my cozy nest. Autumn is a peaceful season of contentment, a time to joyfully revisit gentle domestic arts and embrace familiar routines. As summer days grow shorter, I start to experience that familiar longing for evenings nestled in by the fire, all snug as a bug with a fuzzy blanket, a hot drink in hand, and a book on my lap.

Autumn is a season to reflect on the life we've always dreamed of. Do we have to have the perfect life or dream home to be content right now? Of course not. We have a life worth being grateful for every day. *But do we embrace that life? Do we savor it?* Do we live life to the full this season, or do we spend it in discontent, bemoaning the fact that summer is over or the darkness of winter is on its way? Do we expect to be more content only when or if we buy that new house, have lots of money to decorate, or can work less and have more time to stay home and enjoy life?

Why delay happiness? You are in the perfect season to create a sense of peace and contentment *right now* in your home and your life.

My Autumn Manifesto

Autumn's beauty does not depend on the temperature outside or the turning of the leaves. I don't see it as a precursor to a long, dark, cold winter. Fall is the perfect season to find contentment at home by paying attention to what we already have. The simple daily rituals of homemaking, baking, nesting, decorating, and preparing for the winter holidays ahead create a sense of peace with what we have right in front of us.

Contentment isn't the result of arriving at the latest, greatest, cleanest, trendiest home. All we need is right in front of us. Contentment comes when we embrace the life we can create right now in an authentic, warm, meaningful-from-the-inside-out kind of home. And fall is the perfect season for this because it's a time for nesting and making our home more comfortable and more functional for that inevitable season ahead.

Our winter season in the Pacific Northwest doesn't include many snowstorms, but I still picture myself battening down the hatches in preparation for the storms. No matter what our seasons actually look like, I want my family to feel safe, warm, protected, and prepared for anything.

Autumn sparks the senses. With the first wisps of chimney smoke in the air, I want to sense and feel my surroundings. I don't want to be bombarded by too many expectations in my home. I've always had more fun with the subtle touches and nods to the season than the full-on, crafty, themed sides of seasons and holidays. That's just my style—too much decor or stuff in my house overwhelms me. I get pleasure in the slow nesting process and when cozying up the house.

Fall invites me to add layers of warmth and create inviting spaces for my family to enjoy. Here are a few ideas to do just that: Bring in a rug; add cozy throws to your couch; change pillow covers to soft, warm textures; fill vases with fall branches and bowls with pinecones; rearrange the mantel and bookshelf decor with slightly deeper, richer colors and accessories that reflect the comforts of home; update the dining room with layers of linens, and set the table with a basket of pretty gourds or sunflowers.

In this season, my family renews the rituals of cooking and savoring time in our kitchen. We bring out our favorite chili recipe, make our traditional pumpkin squares, and start dreaming of Thanksgiving dinner. We say goodbye to the unstructured days of summer and return to fall's gentler rhythms and routines. Manageable evolutions work best with my life and probably with yours too. We can avoid the stress of trying to arrive at a final look when we savor the freedom to fluff up our nest as we feel inspired and compose a home we love one pinecone and warm blanket at a time.

Give Yourself a Season of Grace

Personally, I think Christmas should be in January. I mean, January can be kind of a dark and depressing month without much going on to keep our spirits up. It is my birthday month, but that's about the only highlight for me. Thanksgiving and Christmas are over, and spring is so far away. My family has actually discussed moving our Christmas festivities until after the first of the year. Just imagine, everything would be on sale, and we might even get our Christmas cards out on time! That's all I have to say about that. Carry on.

Actually, on a related note (move in a little closer here because I have another random confession), I don't follow that rule about not decorating for Christmas until the day after Thanksgiving. Shhhh! Apparently I believe rebellion is the first step toward sanity.

You see, contrary to when I rush the season, I find myself savoring my days and my experience when I introduce the decor earlier and more gradually. I'm not talking about going crazy and blowing up a plastic Santa for the yard in October. (I'm sorry, there are some decorations I can't make myself endure, even for the kids, no matter what season it is.) I'm simply talking about adding a touch of greenery here and there and some twinkling lights in the middle of November. Maybe I'm weird, but I feel no conflict with the idea of eating turkey dinner and giving thanks for our blessings by a Christmas tree. That scene seems so relaxing and magical and wonderful! If that's a crime, I'm here to turn myself in.

For many years, we didn't put out any Christmas decorations until later in December. We procrastinated so long that on more than one occasion we cut down a Christmas tree under the cover of darkness just moments before the Christmas tree lot closed for the holidays. We aren't lazy—we just tend to do too many things. Our last-minute rush came because we were too frazzled to enjoy the unhurried evolution of the holiday season. We couldn't keep up with ourselves, and our poor kids missed out on some of the traditions we didn't have time for because we tried to fit in too many activities in too little time.

In fact, years ago we felt obligated to go to every event and do everything we were told was required of a young family and a couple in ministry. We rushed our way through Thanksgiving and Christmas as if they were tasks to cross off our to-do list. One might have thought the world would end if we weren't present with a present. It was exhausting.

Trying to fit all I wanted or needed to do in between the two big holidays and being present at ALL THE EVENTS in several locations with ALL THOSE PRESENTS was asking for heartburn. We love getting together with family and friends, but we learned we just can't please everyone all the time or keep up the pace set by unreal expectations. As a gift to our family we decided what traditions were sacred to us and started to just say no to excessive holiday stress.

Give yourself grace about when and how to celebrate each holiday season. Enjoy traditions and time with your family and embrace friends, but don't run yourself ragged trying to please everyone or keep up with everything. Remember the reason for the season, hold on to what matters, and let the rest go (or just consider the extras to be icing on the cake).

Just like the glittery frost sparkles that slowly appear on our front porch this time of year, gently usher in the sparkle, greenery, and festivity at a pace that will make this season beautiful to you and those you love.

Embrace a Natural Christmas

Because I am a less-fuss type of girl when it comes to decorating, I don't haul out a million boxes at once and spend a day or two going to town decorating my house, draping everything in tinsel or sparkle so I can officially start the Christmas season. Nothing wrong with that level of festivity—it's just not my style.

In fact, call me Scrooge, but I sometimes don't even bring out the Christmas decorating storage boxes at all. Gasp! I know. Am I becoming a Christmas minimalist? Not really. But because I like to decorate when I feel inspired, I make things easy on myself and start with nature as my go-to decor in every season. I bring out small touches of Christmas one gentle bit of evergreen at a time.

I keep things simple and natural. Fresh greenery is my favorite because it engages my senses in a way the faux just can't (although I use both real and faux if it strikes my fancy). And if it dries out before December 25, it's easy to replace with a new batch. The Northwest offers plenty of trees and greenery options right outside our door!

What are some of the natural elements you might be able to use in your part of the country? I love the smell of fresh-cut pine and cedar, so it is a treat to walk outside and cut branches to use inside. It's a simple pleasure that I enjoy all winter long.

I may move things around as my whims strike. I may add more or take away some as the season progresses. That's part of the fun of letting decor evolve through the seasons a bit at a time—you can fully enjoy the experience along the way and not be too stressed out when it comes to the actual holiday.

Cherish Sacred Seasonal Memories

Though I definitely like to keep things simple, I don't want to be so focused on simplifying that I abandon sacred traditions, forget what we are celebrating, or neglect to create a festive environment for my family. Even when we crave doing less, a balanced life includes special traditions that help us savor the joy and make wonderful memories to treasure.

Our teenage son, Luke, is our third and last child, and several times my two girls have gently let me know that I let an important family tradition slide. Mom fail! But good for them because they watch out for their brother so he doesn't end up with a childhood void of special family memories! Poor, neglected, third children.

Luke actually keeps us on our toes by getting us out of the house to cut down a Christmas tree. He loves this tradition, and I'm grateful that he shared with us how much it means to him. It's worth the expense of a real tree and the time it takes to get it (and the inevitable near-death experiences of using a saw and then flinging a 12-foot tree onto the top of our car) because it enriches our family's holiday season.

Life with kids in your home will go by in the blink of an eye, but those memories of their relatively few Christmases as a family under one roof will last a lifetime. They are worth keeping alive and happy! The memories. And the family.

It's also important to evolve with our family's needs and seasons of life. Every year is different at our house with our girls getting older. Kylee and Lance are starting their own family traditions, and Courtney is moving out of the house (cue ALL THE TEARS), but we embrace each season as it is, each one fresh and new and equally as wonderful. There is a season for everything. Take each one as it comes and cherish it.

Beat the Winter Blues

So after the holidays, things go a little downhill. Am I right? It's dark. And dark can mean, "I'm quite possibly going to spiral into that blah mood that comes with light deprivation." It's cold, so we are often stuck inside. Short of going to Hawaii to warm up and beat the blues (an idea I would wholeheartedly support), I need to invite certain rituals, habits, and projects into my life to brighten my mood.

Winter has gifts of its own. Besides the opportunity to wear cute scarves and boots, the season offers time to get a lot of home projects and nesting done. In January I start to get extra inspired about what I can do to improve my home in the upcoming months. I make a list of goals and then put the winter months to good use by keeping myself occupied and happy inside the home. It's a great season to paint a room or organize drawers and closets.

Light is really important in the winter, so the routine of turning on the lights as it starts to get dark is especially helpful. Don't forget to add a warm glow to gloomy corners. I love the tradition of lighting candles as evening falls. We won't get depressed by the darkness when flickering

Inspiration for Every Season

- Enjoy the bounty of the season. Fresh and seasonal fruits, vegetables, and traditional recipes break up the monotony of year-round sameness in our diets.

- Pick a few special traditions for each season to enjoy with your family. Include each person's favorite!

- Start a seasonal gratitude journal. Have everyone in the family add pages.

- Create a simple nesting notebook filled with your family traditions, recipes, and decorating ideas for each season.

- Designate a four-shelf unit for special seasonal decorations. Label one shelf for each season and find a separate area for Christmas. Don't store too much.

- Keep decorations simple for the season. A pretty bowl of fruit on the table, pumpkins and gourds in a basket for the entry, or a wreath on the front door can be enough to make a statement.

- Choose your favorite scents for each season and enjoy candles, essential oils, diffusers, boiled spices on the stove, or homemade potpourri and sachets. And don't forget to savor aromas from baking and cooking.

- Enjoy the sounds of the season. Create seasonal playlists and pump up the tunes so you can whistle while you work.

candles lift the ambience from cave-like to cozy and even add a bit of romance to the mood.

Another great way to enjoy wintertime? Delight in the tradition of enjoying a delicious, home-cooked dinner on a winter night. Make it special! Create an evening playlist for dinner and let the kids create menus. You can put the roast in the oven, and your whole house will smell delicious all day. And such a satisfying meal is a gracious invitation to spend the evening around the table.

The Wonder of Winter

Winter is a dazzling wonderland of inspiration. After the holidays, setting pretty tables is even more fun because there are no holiday expectations—only your desire to make the table inviting. The decor doesn't have to be perfect. Just have fun with it!

Our family has a long-standing tradition of playing a board game at dinner, especially on long winter nights. Our game of choice is a wood and marble game called Agitation. The name should really be changed because it sounds upsetting. The game is enjoyable for a couple or a family with kids of various ages.

This season has encouraged other traditions too. My husband has a standing Tuesday-night guy time with Luke. In the winter they often take the marble game (as we call it) with them to a restaurant and play it while they eat meat loaf. It's a little thing, but the little things really are the big things when it comes to seasonal memories. The more you tie a happy memory to a season, the more you will look forward to those same experiences the next year.

Playing a game together (one that doesn't involve a screen) brings the family together for face-to-face laughter and interaction. Passing the time this way is much more memorable than watching a TV show!

What are some traditions and house projects you could plan for in the winter season? Come up with a few things you would love to do, even if it is as simple as making a new winter wreath for the front door every January. Think of both productive ideas and simple family memories you can shape. Seasonal traditions the whole family can look forward to are special gifts.

Get a Spring in Your Step for Summer

I am charmed by the coziness of cooler weather,
but I come alive in different ways when the sun
comes out. I feel the warming effects of the sun-
shine on my shoulders and on my disposition. As
it streams through my window, it inspires me to
clean and freshen everything in sight. Yes, the sun
shows just how dirty our windows and floors are after
the winter, but that's my cue to take action. I want my windows to
sparkle and my floors to shine. The reflection of light rejuvenates me
to make that happen.

After spending fall and winter *adding* layers of comfort, I feel free
as I start *removing* things in the spring and summer. What felt cozy
and warm in my home a few months ago now feels like excess. I start
folding up the throw blankets. I find myself rearranging furniture to
make my rooms feel more open and airy. I pack up some winter accessories and replace them with spring plants, pretty glass bottles, and a
good dose of fresher, brighter colors. The rearrangement of accessories,
shelving decor, pillows, and anything else makes the home feel fresh
and new again.

I am rejuvenated after sweeping the old leaves off the front porch
and bringing out the weather-friendly cushions so we have comfortable places in the sun. I enjoy digging my hands in the dirt (minus
the encounter with the occasional slug) and planting spring pots. I
suddenly get obsessed with making miniature gardens. I don't have a
particularly green thumb, but all we can do is try. Sometimes we fail,
but we can always learn, and often the enjoyment of the journey is
worth the risk.

Season by season, our homes can evolve along with us no matter
where we live. The little ways we find to delight in each season will in
turn inspire us to pour more TLC into the life and home we have.

Savor It

What simple things could you do in this season to more fully love being in your home? *Set some goals to get things started and learn to savor this place and season you are in.*

What are some of your favorite seasonal meals?

What do you want your house to feel like in this season? *Think about what style you want to create and what mood you want to evoke.*

What area of the house could use a little seasonal spruce up?

CHAPTER 13

Be Happy at Home

But every house where Love abides
And Friendship is a guest,
Is surely home, and home, sweet, home;
For there the heart can rest.
HENRY VAN DYKE

Most of us grew up with fairy tales. We envision how the story is supposed to end—you know, the "happily ever after" part. The prince and princess ride off on the white horse up to the castle (of course). But we know that in real life, there's a lot more to the story than the happily ever after.

A few years ago, things weren't exactly looking like a fairy tale around our house. Our move to Washington wasn't easy, and the story included a few unexpected twists and turns. In those early years of starting the church, we juggled finances just to be able to make our house payment and keep the church doors open long enough for it to get established.

I often had to make tough decisions about which bills to pay first. I avoided answering my telephone because the collection agencies kept calling about unpaid medical bills. A couple of times I opened our front door to find a cheery, bright-yellow door hanger letting me know our electricity would be shut off if I didn't make a payment on our account by the end of the week. Awesome.

It was hard. We were discouraged at times. The nice things we wanted to do for our family had to wait. And the things I wanted to do around my house definitely had to be set aside. Our story was not going as planned. I was certain our days in the new house were numbered, yet I was pretty sure we couldn't even afford to move.

We really didn't know what to do except move forward in faith, believing all things would work together for good. On the surface, I felt at times as if our life might be slowly coming apart at the seams. Even though I knew God was in control, I wondered if this story would not end well (or at least not the way I had hoped it would). On the bright side, I had lots of opportunities to practice trust and faith in those uncertain times!

Just as the most difficult season seemed to be winding down and life finally appeared to be rounding a corner to a season of more stable and comfortable days, I got a call from my aunt letting me know my mom was in an ambulance on the way to the hospital with a rare case of pneumonia that was difficult to treat. I was at home in Washington, and my mom was in Portland. I was three hours away. My heart sank, and my mind raced with potentially dreadful outcomes.

Tears welled up in my eyes, and fear gripped my body as I read a text message from my sister Heather, who was by my mom's side when an ambulance took her to the ER. The text simply said, "Come." I called my sister immediately and screamed, "What does that mean?" Through her tears, she told me my mom could not breathe.

I prayed for God's mercy on her, and as I drove to Portland, a peace came over me that I cannot describe. My sister had specifically told me not to cry all the way there. I was grateful for that feeling of peace so I could focus on the road.

For the next ten days, I sat and slept curled up on a small chair in my mom's hospital room. I watched her every breath and followed her oxygen levels on the monitor next to her bed. Mom had many close calls, and I had many sleepless nights, but somehow she miraculously pulled through and was able to return home. She was weak but alive. I was so grateful for that gift.

As much as I fear those twists and turns in the story of life, they often offer new perspective on what happiness and contentment are all about. I consider those changes in view and priority to be the gifts of such difficult times.

Trying on New Perspectacles

As I got in the car and put on my driving glasses to make the jour-ney home after those stressful two weeks, I was more keenly aware of every blessing around me. The sun felt warm and soothing as it shone down through my dirty, chipped windshield. I sang out loud as my favorite song played over my crackling speakers. Even the familiar smell of our eleven-year-old minivan comforted me. (It was probably the smell of beloved dogs and entire childhoods' worth of spills on our upholstery—even *that* scent was a gift!)

I was struck by how much I had to be grateful for. Especially the double-tall caramel macchiato I had just ordered at Starbucks (even though the name Marsha was written across the cup in a big, black Sharpie).

When we have a fresh perspective on little things all around us—gifts and moments and imperfections that brush right past us in the rush of navigating the everyday—we realize they aren't *little* things at all. They are really the *big* things. They are the signs of a blessed life, the essentials that make us feel alive when we pay attention to them. Like breathing.

We are never promised a fairy-tale ending. But even if the story isn't exactly what we would choose, we can *always* find ways to live more happily every day by embracing the gifts we have right in front of us.

Cultivating Happiness

When you have been away a long time and finally return home, does your house somehow feel different and yet comfortably familiar? As I arrived home after that long drive and turned the key to my front door, I was so happy to be home. I didn't even care that a familiar paper notice on the front door welcomed me home with a reminder to pay our water bill. (Thank you, City, for the reminder. I'm grateful that I will have water once I pay our bill.)

I walked in the house less overwhelmed by unfinished projects (opportunities!), including the swine-colored walls and the smelly

Blogger *Home* ♥ *Love* Story

Happiness in the Making

After living in three different rentals in four years, I realized the importance of simply "making home" even if I was tempted to wait until I had the sofa I was hoping for or those extra five frames I might come across at a yard sale. I realized that if I lived in a rental for a year but left my wall art stacked behind the sofa, waiting for the perfect time to be hung and enjoyed, that meant that our home would be unhomey for 25 percent of the time we lived there. What a waste.

I chose to embrace where our family lived and homify it right then, in the midst of the imperfection. In the process of creating a home right where I was, I found I was learning to love the home we were in.

—Myquillyn Smith,
of the blog Nesting Place

carpet. I was grateful to be home. To hug my family. To see my coffeemaker. To sleep in my own bed. It was all still there, imperfect and wonderful, ready and waiting for me. I was home.

Happiness with our home is possible—and not just when we get what we want. It isn't a feeling that arises only when the house is all furnished or decorated or the bills are finally paid. (Although we are pretty happy with those things, of course!) Happiness comes when we awaken to what we have already. Do you see the blessings in the home you have right now, even in the undone, the waiting, and the apparent setbacks? Gifts are offered to us every day. We are so much happier when we make the most of what we have and remember to open our eyes to see how blessed we really are. That is a lesson that keeps coming back to me.

We have many everyday opportunities to experience more contentment and happiness at home. On the surface, the details might seem small or even insignificant, but through the gift of our senses, we can elevate even the most ordinary experience into something more.

Our surroundings have a significant influence on our attitudes and the way we feel, so investing ourselves in the art of cultivating happiness at home in as many ways as we can is worth the effort. When our home feels right to us, our contentment and happiness will grow even more. As contentment grows, we are stronger and more aware of our blessings when the storms come.

Engaging Your Senses

For our home to really speak to us and encourage us on an emotional level, we want to engage all of our senses in a way that is pleasant, awakens good memories, and nurtures contentment.

We are all moved in different ways by our senses. We can easily take for granted the gifts of sight, touch, smell, hearing, and taste. As we rush through our days, accomplishing all that we feel must be done, we don't often pause to take in the simple beauty around us or deeply breathe in the fresh air that will rejuvenate us.

Senses powerfully enhance our life and surroundings. Remember how unnerved I was with some of the original sights, sounds, and scents of the castle? Or how uncomfortable I felt with the unfortunate color of swine on my walls in my current house? My responses weren't symptoms of discontent—they were little nudges to find the right balance in my home.

Which of your senses are giving you the nudge to make some adjustments and transform your surroundings? Paying close attention to those features that trigger your senses will help you create the home you love, and you'll be happier in the process.

Sight

Some people are happiest when surrounded by colors, patterns, and shapes. They notice everything around them in all its splendor and texture. The way the light casts a shadow or illuminates a painting sends chills up their spine!

Look around your home and other environments to notice which details make your eyes light up and cause you to pause and appreciate them. If anything you see in your home makes you want to avert your eyes, find a creative resolution so you can enjoy your home from every angle. And when you are elsewhere, notice which colors or touches of beauty capture your attention. Maybe you can recreate them in your personal spaces.

To heighten your visual delight throughout your home, incorporate attractive paint colors and fabrics, and include various shapes of furnishings and accessories. If you are invigorated by color or pattern, the elements you add to your home can serve a visual feast for your eyes.

On the other hand, carefully selected colors and textures can also help you create a sense of calm in your home. By replacing a riot of pattern and contrast with simplicity and unity, you offer your eyes rest and your spirit a place for personal retreat.

Paint colors can set a personal, pleasant ambience in a room. Even though I love many colors, for the sake of my sanity at home I keep my wall colors in the main rooms of my house to soft and varied shades of warm grays that flow easily from room to room. The subtle flow of neutral colors sets the mood for our home and allows me to have fun with color and pattern in other ways.

Touch

Some people instinctively reach out to touch everything. They want to feel the texture of a fabric or the smoothness of a stone. Every fabric, accessory, floor covering, counter material, or furnishing can add a little bit more to our experience at home.

Pay attention to textures as you make decorating decisions and collect accessories. What textures do want to have in your home? The warm patina of antiques, hand-crafted furniture or decor pieces, and raw elements add so much character. The unaffected beauty of wood, stone, natural fabrics, and plants provides an authentic ambience.

Beautiful textures will present your home as warm, relaxed, and accessible. To heighten the tactile experience of your home, pair a variety of opposite textures together. Rough with smooth. Shiny with dull. Woven with silky.

Add plump, down-filled pillows to your sofas, and drape soft blankets over the backs of chairs. A wool or natural-fiber rug can provide a great foundation for a conversation area and also cover up less-than-beautiful carpet so your seating area will feel more inviting. (Yes, you can layer an area rug over your wall-to-wall carpet. Use a thin rug pad to keep the area rug from creeping.)

Give yourself the gift of happiness through texture in every room. Luxurious sheets for your bedrooms and stacks of soft, fluffy towels to make your bathroom feel like a spa! Small details have a big impact on our day-to-day experience at home.

Smell

Some people have a keen sense of smell and associate vivid memories with different scents. The smell of lilac transports them to their grandma's garden. The yummy goodness of fresh-baked bread makes them feel at home anywhere.

Basic cleanliness will go a long way toward a fresh, clean-smelling home. If you go through the main checklist, you will keep your home's scent inviting: Dust, do the dishes, clean out the refrigerator, keep up on laundry, wash sheets, and clean bathrooms and bedrooms regularly.

Why not make your own signature scent? I love simmering spiced cider on the stove and baking cookies for the scent of yummy comfort. I light candles in the evening to create an inviting ambience and to infuse our home with relaxing scents. As part of my morning routine, I enjoy walking around my house with my spray bottle, spritzing sheets and bedrooms with invigorating essential oils.

Style Notes

Create your own signature scents at home with essential oils. Fill a clean spray bottle with a cup of warm water and four or more drops of your favorite oil (or a blend of oils). Spray your bedding, carpet, pillows, curtains, or furniture to freshen up the room without harmful chemicals. Have fun changing the scent for the seasons or your moods. Some fall and winter favorite oils are vanilla, nutmeg, orange, cinnamon, and clove. In the summer, treat yourself to the scent of lemon, lime, grapefruit, geranium, or lavender.

My husband loves for our home to smell like vanilla, nutmeg, and cloves, so we kept those cozy scents going all winter long. In the summer I come alive with the combined scents of lemon verbena, jasmine, and orange!

If you have a family, it's a good idea to do a scratch-and-sniff test with them before you get too spritz-happy with a new scent. Because we are all so different, you want to be sure that your "aah" is not another person's "ugh."

If you are sensitive to smells, use unscented natural laundry soaps for sheets and clothing. The clean, fresh scent of your home can encourage you to take a deep breath and relax, but the wrong scents can make you want to plug your nose and run outside.

Find a pleasing scent you love and make it a part of your daily routines.

Hearing

Sound reaches people through their ears, but it impacts them in their heart and soul. We are soothed by the sounds of water, the whir of a fan, the soft gentle breeze blowing through the trees. We become energized when music and laughter fill a room. Depending on one's preferences, different styles of music can relax, inspire, or distract us.

Too many sounds at once or at high volumes can agitate.

I'm very sensitive to sound. I'm also an introvert, so even too much conversation drains my energy. (Confession: Even though I am an introvert, I talk a lot, so I can wear out my own ears!) I cringe at jarring sounds, like my dog Jack barking at the window, but the sound of the waves soothes me. I'm pretty sure this means I should live in a beach house overlooking water.

Consider your tolerance to sound and embrace your preferences as you set the tone and volume of your home's unique soundtrack. Knowing how sound impacts me, I carve out periods of silence during my day so my ears can rest and my soul can feel rejuvenated. I retreat to my room or even the shower when I need peace and quiet.

To enhance your emotional connection to your home, select sources for sounds you enjoy—from a simple water fountain on the front porch to a favorite music playlist.

Taste

Okay, are you a foodie? If so, you know that tasting a delicious marinara sauce or savoring a piece of fine chocolate can make your heart sing and all your senses come alive! Our physical sense of taste isn't something most of us consider when we make decorating decisions, but the way we prepare meals and experience the comfort of food can give us clues about the way we prepare our homes and experience comfort there.

Your morning coffee ritual is the perfect example. And if you are a tea lover, all the same delights apply! A coffee ritual can become a way to savor all of your senses and set the tone for the day or be a reset button in the afternoon. It's a ritual based on physical taste…and yet it becomes an experience for all the senses.

Sense of Well-Being

As you find ways to feed the senses in your home, pay special attention to the ambience of your kitchen. Intentionally or unintentionally, your kitchen sets the tone for how you and your family give and receive food. So let's be intentional. What decor change or cleaning frenzy might improve the message your kitchen sends? If its chaos says,

Delighting the Senses

That first cup of coffee can get you going in the morning and get ideas brewing for how to cultivate happiness at home sip by sip.

- *Scent.* Wake up and smell the coffee, right? There's nothing like inhaling the scent of fresh-brewed coffee.

- *Sight and touch.* Choose a favorite mug. As you pour your coffee, pause long enough to hold the pretty coffee mug and savor the warmth. If you add a bit of cream, watch the swirl of the milk blend with the coffee to create the rich color of caramel.

- *Sound.* Appreciate the stillness and quiet of the morning. Enjoy one of the first sounds of your day—the soft gurgle of coffee filling your ceramic cup.

- *Taste.* What flavors do you taste in that first sip? How does this taste actually lift your mood?

You lose all these experiences when you gulp down your coffee from a paper cup on the way out the door! Lingering over your coffee takes only a few moments, but they are moments well spent.

"Hurry, eat, and get out of here," figure out a way to have it say, "Enjoy, sip, savor, and stay awhile." Once the message changes, you will be less likely to grab fast food on the way home from work and more likely to keep a few delicious, easy-to-prepare options on hand.

If you do pick up dinner on the way home, serve it at the table—even when that is a table for one. Disconnect from phones and other forms of media and engage with the pleasure of nourishment. Treat yourself to meals that will satisfy your taste buds and your deeper hunger for peace and comfort. Make sit-down dinners a priority so you can fully engage with your meal, savoring the entire process. Pause before meals to offer thanks. It's amazing how simply pausing for a moment of gratitude can transform the little we have into more than enough.

There's No Place like Home

One early morning back in the castle, Jerry and I were getting ready to leave on a plane for a church-planters' conference. It was still dark outside as I was putting the suitcases in the entry by the front door. Out of the corner of my eye, I caught a glimpse of something small and furry running down the hallway. *Oh my gosh, please tell me that was not a rat.* I had to do a double take. It was painfully early, and I hadn't had my coffee yet. *Um, it had eyes. It was furry. And it was running.* Definitely a rodent.

After screaming at the top of my lungs for Jerry to come save me, I realized I *recognized* that rodent. He wasn't just any common old house rat—he was our furry hamster, Cheddar (Cheds for short). Yet because I will not touch ANYTHING that resembles a rodent, even if it is a family member, Jerry needed to corner and catch him. Just as Jerry reached for duct tape to secure Cheds inside (well, we wouldn't duct tape *him*, but the place where he chewed through his cage), we heard a big *boom*. Then the house went pitch black. Taking full advantage of the darkness, Cheds was able to escape again! Did Cheds orchestrate his own perfect escape? I wondered.

While fumbling around for a flashlight and crawling on hands and knees trying to find Cheds, we were completely unaware of a serious drama unfolding just up the hill—our neighbor's entire house was literally slipping out from under her.

At five thirty that morning, our neighbor had awakened to a loud cracking sound. Before she could get outside to safety, her beautiful home overlooking the city started crumbling all around her, sliding down the hillside, busting into bits and taking a couple other houses

Five Ways to Be Happier

1. *Create a happy place.*
If you feel as if your home is falling apart at the seams, give yourself an afternoon to create one happy place. Clear the clutter. Add something pretty. Turn on some music. Light a candle. Sit back and enjoy your happy place.

2. *Find your attitude of gratitude.*
Slow down to make note of blessings. I'm a big believer in making gratitude lists. I also keep a list of people to pray for throughout the day to focus my mind on others and on God's presence in all circumstances.

3. *Go back to the basics.*
If you are starting to lose your zeal for your home, go back to basics. Dream a little. Invite friends over. Engage your senses. Remind yourself of the simple routines and rhythms that encourage you.

4. *Choose joy.*
What are twenty little things you could look forward to this season? Five things you could look forward to this week? Or one thing you could enjoy today? I display the words "Choose Joy" on a chalkboard to remind myself that happiness is a choice.

5. *Reset the day.*
Leaving the source of the stress for a few moments can change your disposition. Take a walk outside, bring a cup of coffee out on the porch, take time for solitude and prayer, or indulge in window shopping to reset the day toward happiness. And of course, chocolate always helps.

along with it. Water lines broke and power lines snapped. Friends across the street from this unfolding disaster heard the ruckus and ran outside. They rescued the homeowner with a ladder as she clung to chunks of her house that stopped short of the giant heap of rubble near our house.

Moments before, we were focused on the inconvenience of nearly missing our flight due to a runaway rodent. Meanwhile, our neighbor was watching everything she had crumble before her eyes. I can't imagine the horror she experienced that morning.

When my husband and I returned home from our trip, we examined the site of the tragedy. Instead of our neighbor's lovely home—a place where we had hung out for block parties—there was a gaping hole of dirt. Her lot was completely gone. In the ravine far below, windows, cars, doors, chunks of housing materials, and personal belongings were scattered in a heap.

You can't see something like that pile of rubble and not step back and think, *What do I truly value? What if everything I have was stripped away from me, snatched from my hands, and tossed onto a mountain of debris? What's important to have in life, and what can I do without? How would I cope with something like this?* Such a happening changes one's focus. We were grateful to still have a home, and our neighbor was certainly grateful to be alive. Perspective changes everything, doesn't it?

Do we have faith that we are right where we are supposed to be, at this address, in this house? Do we trust that we have been given exactly what we need to be content today? Do we recognize the blessings of the house we already have, even if we have to search for happiness in the challenges? And if we are living what most people perceive as the good life, could we find happiness and contentment with less?

We can get so caught up in our own four walls and the imperfections that seem to surround us, can't we? We have so much to be grateful for. Often what we have is what someone else is dreaming about. When we have the right perspective, we realize the life and home of our dreams is possible *right where we are.* Finding joy in the smallest details and the greater purpose of creating a home will bring us the sense of happiness and contentment we long for.

The opportunity to love the home we have is a gift. And at the end of the day, no matter where we live, the truth remains—there's no place like home.

Tell Me Your Story

Creating a home is like writing a never-ending love story. And every chapter of our life brings a fresh perspective. *How can the home you have be a part of your happily-ever-after story?*

If you have done the 31-Day Love Your Home Challenge along the way, what is the biggest change you've experienced?

If you are about to begin the challenge in the pages that follow, enjoy! *Pay attention to the way your affection for your home and your life grows.*

Tell me your home love story. Go to lovethehomeyouhave.com to find inspiration, free downloads, resources, and a community of others who are eager to encourage one another. Create and share your home love story and read others at homelovestories.com. *I can't wait to hear your story!*

31-DAY

Love Your Home

CHALLENGE

{ HOME GRATITUDE }

Your home is a gift and a blessing. Walk around your house and think about how thankful you are for a roof over your head. In spite of all its quirks and imperfections, your home is where you can create a place to nurture yourself and bless your family. Try not to worry about all the material things you want to buy or change or improve. Instead, remember how blessed you are to be able to create a home full of memories with what you already have. View each room through the lens of gratitude for the life you can create and memories you can make in your home!

What room or memory stands out as a blessing today?

_____

_____

{ DECLUTTER }

What's the very first spot that comes to mind when you think of the most cluttered drawer or closet in your home? The kitchen drawer full of junk you never use? The closet with an avalanche of clothes? Clutter takes up space, making daily routines more challenging. Give yourself the gift of a less cluttered life. Choose one small area you can tackle today. Turn on some music and create order in one spot in your home!

Which area did you declutter? How did you feel while taking this step toward organization?

_____

_____

{ LESS IS MORE }

When horizontal spaces are clean, you feel better about the whole house. Today, concentrate only on the horizontal surfaces in your home. Room by room, clear clutter, remove excess decor (box up, put away, or give away), polish the tabletops and shelves, and sweep the floors. If doing this throughout the house is too overwhelming, choose one room and make the surfaces shine. Go with the less-is-more mindset for a while and see what a difference clean floors and uncluttered surfaces can make!

Going forward, what surface could you designate as clutter free?

_____

_____

{ MAKE IT PRETTY }

A messy kitchen can ruin your whole day. You know what I'm talking about! No one is happy when dirty dishes are stacked all over the counters. Set aside 15 minutes today to show your kitchen some love. Clear your counters, polish up your faucet, and remove all the fingerprints from your appliances, cabinet faces, and hardware. Take a look at what's on your counter. Is it useful? Is it attractive? Is it in a convenient spot? You'll wake up tomorrow much happier with a clean kitchen!

How did you feel after giving your kitchen a little love?

_____

_____

{ DELIGHT YOUR SENSES }

Pleasing our senses will make our homes feel inviting, nourishing, and full of pleasant memories. What does your home smell like right now? Even if you're sensitive to scents, consider keeping your home fresh and clean in nonchemical ways. Throw open the windows, empty old food from the fridge, take out the garbage, wash sheets, dust tables, and vacuum rugs. Then light a candle or bake some cookies!

What is your favorite memory associated with a beautiful scent? Perhaps that could become one of your signature home scents.

_____

_____

{ EMBRACE A MEMORY }

In our fast-paced life, time goes by too quickly. Think about a recent moment you don't want to forget. Maybe your kids said something funny yesterday or your husband brought home a sweet gift for you. Maybe a friend sent you a kind note or you prepared a fun meal for your family. Take some time to write down the details, print off a picture, or draw a sketch to remind yourself of the good times in life and embrace the happy memories you are creating for yourself and your family.

What do you hope to remember from this very day?

_____

_____

{ YOUR SANCTUARY }

Many times our bedrooms turn into dumping grounds for everything from laundry to odds and ends we don't know what to do with. We all deserve a bedroom that is a sanctuary from the world, not a storage room. Start a new habit to make your bed every day. We're less likely to allow our beds to be taken over with clutter when they are pretty and made. Take a moment to look at your bedroom and see what you could improve using what you already have. Tidy up, remove clutter, and see how much better your room will feel!

What does "sanctuary" mean to you?

_____

_____

{ PAMPER YOURSELF }

You can easily get discouraged about life when you don't take care of yourself. Do something special just for you today. Run a bubble bath, go for a walk, paint your nails, or stop in a local café and find a great corner to savor a delicious coffee and a good book.

How do you feel when you spend time on you and your interests?

_____

_____

_____

_____

{ A HOME NOTEBOOK }

Choose a three-ring notebook to hold your inspiration photos and notes about your home. Make dividers for each room in the house. Add plastic sleeves for magazine photos. Draw arrows and add notes of details about *why* you like your inspiration photos. Keep notes of maintenance records or paint colors or project planning.

What dreams and goals come to mind as you start creating your notebook?

_____

_____

{ RECLAIM THE DINING ROOM }

Formal dining rooms may not be as popular as they used to be, but let's not lose sight of the importance of creating memories around the table. Is your table covered with papers and random dishes? Today is the day to reclaim your dining room as a place for conversation, good food, and memory making. Once the room and table are clutter free, put together a fun centerpiece using a bowl or tray filled with items you find around the house. In the summer, fill the bowl with seasonal fruit. In the fall, you could fill your bowl or even a round wreath with items like pinecones, pumpkins, or squash. At Christmastime, fill the bowl with ornaments. In the winter use green apples, pears, or artichokes for a pretty and simple centerpiece.

What centerpiece might inspire you and your family this month?

_____

_____

{ Fresh Flowers }

Every room will feel so much better with a touch of life—plants or flowers or other organic elements, such as fruits, vegetables, or branches. What organic elements do you have in your home? You can cut branches from your yard, try growing plants (such as succulents or herbs) in your window, or treat yourself to an inexpensive weekly bouquet from the market.

How do you want to bring the beauty of nature in to your home?

_____

_____

_____

{ A Note to Self }

Encouragement from others can be wonderful, but you can also speak kindly to yourself by gathering favorite quotes, Bible verses, or uplifting thoughts. Post your favorites on your bulletin board or a place where you may unexpectedly run across them.

What message does your heart need right now?

_____

_____

_____

_____

{ DRESS IT UP }

Even if you are just planning on macaroni and cheese tonight, make dinner a fun and memorable event. If you have kids, let them write out the menu and set the table, or set a pretty table yourself with your favorite dishes. Get dressed up, play some fancy background music, and sit around the table together to enjoy one another's company. Add a few memorable family meal ideas to your calendar. Get creative! DIY pizza night? Cookie decorating after dinner?

What are three ways you could dress up dinnertime at your house?

_____

_____

_____

{ WELCOME HOME }

What does your front door say to you when you walk up to it each day? If it doesn't say "welcome home" in a way that makes you smile, today would be a good day to tidy up a bit. Sweep off the porch, clean up around the door, and maybe plant a pot of flowers or make a seasonal wreath. Make it cheery and welcoming!

How will you change the message shared by your front porch, door, or entry?

_____

_____

_____

{ MAKING MEMORIES }

When was the last time you restocked your frames with new family photos? Take a few moments to look through your phone and camera today for some fun, frame-worthy candid family memories and send them to be printed. Pick them up and put them in frames. Your family will feel loved every time they pass by the family photos!

As you selected new photos, which image brought a smile to your face?

_____

_____

_____

DAY 16

{ A PLACE OF YOUR OWN }

Do you have a cozy spot in your house to call your own? Pull together a comfy chair, a lamp, and a footstool. Gather up a few favorite books or magazines. Create a special place that inspires you to enjoy quiet time or dream time every day.

What might you daydream about in your new, personal nook?

_____

_____

_____

_____

{ LOVELY LINENS }

I t's time to clean out the linen closet. If you have too many linens or a collection of old, ugly, or worn sheets that aren't comfortable or don't fit any current beds, designate today as the day to pare down to your favorites. I have only one set of sheets for my bedroom. I buy only linens I really love, and they can be fairly expensive. So instead of purchasing and storing multiple sheets, I just wash, dry, and put them back on the same day.

Which linen item could you update or upgrade to bring beauty to your bedroom?

_____

_____

_____

{ A GRACIOUS GIVER }

S et up a wrapping and gift station. Be the gift giver or note writer you'd like to be—at a moment's notice. Designate a gift closet or drawer for collecting pretty gift bags, paper, tape, and small cards so you're ready to treat a special someone to a gift that's hand wrapped with your unique signature touch.

How do you feel when you give to others? When you receive from others?

_____

_____

_____

_____

{ Make It Sparkle }

It's time to restore order in the bathroom. Pick an area in this hard-working space today to refresh—a drawer, your makeup bag, or a medicine cabinet. Toss out the old, expired, or unused items. Wipe out shelves and drawers and reorganize and revamp containers. Step back and enjoy your sparkling space!

How will a cleaner bathroom improve your day?

_____

_____

_____

{ Music to Your Soul }

Do you have a soundtrack for your home? Music can remind you of happy memories and change your mood dramatically. Today give your family the gift of a great mood through music! Create a special playlist for everything you do in your home, including relaxing, celebrating, dining, and even cleaning.

What genre of music gives joy to your family?

_____

_____

_____

_____

{ A CLEANING FRENZY }

We all know the feeling of looking around our house in horror because everything is out of control. Restoring order might seem overwhelming, but oftentimes a quick 15-minute cleaning frenzy is all you need to get on the road to peace. Focus on one corner you think you can make look better (not perfect) in only 15 minutes. Take a before photo, set a timer, and challenge yourself to a speedy, 15-minute transformation. When you're finished, take another photo. Feeling better? I thought so!

Which corner are you most excited to see in its "after" version?

_____

_____

{ TWENTY LITTLE THINGS }

Sometimes we get so caught up in the big things we want out of life or for our home that we fail to be grateful for things that we already have. Make a list of 20 little things you love about your life at home and why they matter to you. Post the list or put it in your journal or home notebook. Read through it often and add to it whenever you are reminded of something else you love. I dare you to stop at 20 things you love!

How have you noticed your gratitude deepening while doing the 31-Day Love Your Home Challenge?

_____

_____

{ HAPPY SURPRISES }

The littlest things can bring joy to our day. Today, line the dresser or desk drawer you use most often with fun scrapbook paper or pretty wrapping paper. You could even add a small scented sachet or soap to awaken your senses.

Which patterns and colors boost your happiness in this life season?

DAY 24

{ YOUR HANDBAG }

A well-organized purse will transform daily tasks, such as grocery shopping, running errands, or trying to find your cell phone in the dark abyss of your handbag. No one likes to sort through receipts stuck together with gum or have crackers fall out of her makeup bag while searching for lipstick. Today would be a great day to toss out all the trash and old receipts. Use cute zippered pouches to contain and organize makeup and receipts. Add a small pocket-size notebook for jotting down notes, thoughts, and inspiration. An organized handbag can reduce stress and set you up for success. My friend Mary has a hook on her purse for keys so she can always find them. That small hook is a happiness booster and a stress reducer!

How does finding what you need when you need it change the way you feel and function?

{ LIVING-ROOM WISH LIST }

How do you feel when you walk into your living room? Do you enjoy spending time there? If you're just getting started with your home, resist becoming overwhelmed with design details. You need only a few basic things to create a comfortable room—a place to sit, a surface to set a cup on, a lamp or two for ambience and function, and furniture in close proximity for conversation. Once you have the basics covered, start to add new layers, such as a fun pillow, a pretty throw, a rug, or accessories like a bouquet or a stack of books to inspire cozy times. Start your living-room wish list and put it in your home notebook.

What is the next thing you'd like to add to your living room?

_____

_____

{ MAKE IT HAPPEN }

Those nagging projects that hang over your head can steal your joy, leaving you feeling overwhelmed, uninspired, and discontent. Pick one project you can make progress on or even finish today. Celebrate your progress!

As you complete one of these nagging projects, what are you feeling—relief, joy, lightness, courage, pride, freedom? Savor the feeling of accomplishment!

_____

_____

_____

{ ORDER IN THE KITCHEN }

Whether you store your food or baking supplies in a large pantry or a small cabinet, today is the day to throw out unneeded items, repackage bulk goods, and label containers to get organized. Make food preparation a breeze by placing a plastic bin or a basket in your refrigerator for lunch or snack items.

How does organizing the kitchen increase your love and acceptance of your home?

_____

_____

{ YOUR COLOR PERSONALITY }

Spend some time today thinking about your favorite colors. Surrounding yourself with shades that make you feel happy and alive can change the way you feel about your home. Start a search for a color family that makes your heart sing. Search for complementary palettes on Pinterest or tear out magazine pages of rooms draped in tones you love. Are those colors in your house? Think about how those colors make you feel and how you might be able to incorporate them in your rooms. Even if you can't imagine painting walls or changing your furniture right now, you can add colors you love with drawer liners, clothing, pillow covers, books, and even flowers. Add your favorite palette inspiration to your home notebook.

Which colors seem to spark your imagination or change your attitude?

_____

_____

{ Your Purpose Statement }

Contentment is easier to find when you identify what matters most to you. Write a purpose statement for your family and home that will help you keep your focus. You will likely find that what you desire most is not the designer look or the perfect house but the love of family and the comfort of home. You can write your purpose statement on a chalkboard or get fancy and have it printed and framed or turned into an art canvas. Go to lovethehomeyouhave.com to find lots of ideas and support as you create and commit to your purpose statement. Don't forget to share your home love story and read others at homelovestories.com.

How might writing your purpose statement help you live it out?

_____

_____

{ Paint Something }

Paint can revive just about anything. Select a piece of furniture or a small accessory, like a lackluster candlestick that needs a fresh, new color. Search your favorite blogs for painting tips or inspiration. Take your before photo, gather your supplies, and get started! Don't forget to take your after photo once you've transformed it into something more beautiful.

How does reviving an object with color also revive your connection to your home?

_____

_____

{ UNPLUG }

The online world can be addicting and distracting from the life you really want to live. Dare to ignore your cell phone, your TV, and your computer today. Live more fully, be in the moment, and embrace the people and needs that come across your path today. Do you feel less stressed and frazzled at the end of the day? Write your observations in your journal or home notebook.

How might unplugging specifically help your home become a refuge for you and your family?

_____

_____

_____

Notes

1. Emily P. Freeman, *A Million Little Ways* (Grand Rapids: Revell, 2013), 16.

2. Gary Chapman, *The Five Love Languages* (Chicago: Northfield, 1995).

3. Charles Duhigg, *The Power of Habit* (New York: Random House, 2012), 109.

Personal Notes

_____

_____

_____

_____

_____

_____

_____

_____

_____

_____

_____

_____

_____

_____

_____

_____

Personal Notes

_____

_____

_____

_____

_____

_____

_____

_____

_____

_____

_____

_____

_____

_____

_____

_____

Personal Notes

_____

_____

_____

_____

_____

_____

_____

_____

_____

_____

_____

_____

_____

_____

_____

_____

Personal Notes

Discover more ways to love your home.

Join Melissa for this unique, beautiful tour of her inspiring home and ideas.

The Inspired Room

The eagerly anticipated, lavishly illustrated "book" experience of Melissa Michaels' celebrated blog, The Inspired Room, is here. If you're a longtime fan of her personable style or a fellow lover of pretty, real-life decor, you'll delight in this full-color tour of Melissa's home and favorite family spaces alongside room-by-room ideas.

Step inside as Melissa shares lessons learned when turning her house into a home, plenty of inspiring photos, and encouraging insights to help you embrace your authentic style through:

- doable improvements for every room
- attainable decorating, organizational, and DIY solutions
- transforming tips for lighting, color, and style
- ways to reclaim small or unique areas

Best of all, you don't need a big budget or perfect DIY skills to embrace Melissa's practical home decor philosophy. You'll return to this book again and again for inspiration to fall in love with the home you have.

Acknowledgments

I feel incredibly blessed by so many who have shaped this dream in the many years it was being lived and written. Without you, this book would never have come to life.

Thank you...

To The Inspired Room blog community (the real-life friends who happen to live in my computer) for being with me through this wild journey of home loving, blogging, and book writing. Your friendship, sense of humor, support, and encouragement along the way has changed my life and is a gift for which I will be forever grateful. Thank you.

To my husband for sharing these crazy adventures with me, for better or worse, for richer or poorer. There is no one I'd rather make a home with than you.

To my daughters, Courtney and Kylee, who make creating a home a joy and writing a book a much less scary and lonely endeavor. Everything you are a part of is far lovelier and more fun than I could have dreamed.

To my son, Luke, who makes me laugh when he gives me the side-eye as I do crazy things like hang driftwood curtain rods in his room or add yet another giant pillow to the sectional. Thank you for putting up with those questionable additions to our home. I hope your wife will thank me someday. PS. You are my favorite.

To my dad for driving me around neighborhoods in search of fairy-tale castles, chasing rodents out of every house, investing in many of my grand ideas, and for never once making me question that my dreams might come true.

To my mom, who shares my love of making any house a home. Without her willingness to strip wallpaper, bargain hunt, and make curtains (and even to risk falling off ladders to hang them) my homes would not have been nearly as cozy or memorable to create.

To my sister, Heather, who enthusiastically supports so many of my endeavors and offers wisdom on all things book design. I am especially grateful for the fun memories we share of adventures abroad and at home with small people.

To my friends far and near who helped plant dreams and pull weeds, paint furniture and swine-colored walls, brought goodies and laughter, and graciously opened your homes and hearts over the years. Thank you for being an inspiration in true friendship and hospitality.

To the girls from the DIY Diva blogging group who not only challenge me to try new things, but generously offer support and advice on everything from business decisions to taking better photos to how to use power tools without dying.

To the (in)courage sisters for doing what you all do so bravely and encouraging the rest of us to find courage to do the same.

To the many friends along the way who encouraged me to write, especially my lovely soul-sister, Ann, who cheered me on and gave confidence to this reluctant introverted writer to take the risk of crafting a book proposal. I'm forever grateful.

To my literary agents, Bill and Ruth, for representing my work and believing in what I do and what God could do through the stories of creating a home.

To the wonderful team at Harvest House who saw a message of hope in my words and helped transform my rough ideas into a beautiful little package of love for my readers.

And lastly but most importantly, I'm thankful to God for surprising me with that unmistakable nudge so many years ago to step out of my comfortable nest, to use the gifts He gave me to encourage others, and to embrace contentment right where I was.

About the Author

Melissa Michaels is the DIY-challenged creator and author of the popular home decorating blog The Inspired Room, which inspires women to love the home they have. Since 2007 Melissa has been encouraging hundreds of thousands of readers a month with daily posts and inspiration for all things house and home. The Inspired Room was voted as the *Better Homes and Gardens* magazine Reader's Choice decorating blog, and the magazine editors selected it as one of their five favorite decorating blogs in 2014.

Melissa lives with her husband, Jerry, their son, Luke, and two impossibly adorable Doodle pups, Jack and Lily, whose adventures are well-loved and followed on their blog (theinspireddogblog.com) and Facebook page (Facebook.com/jack.goldendoodle). The Michaels' daughters, Courtney and Kylee (and her husband, Lance), are an active part of The Inspired Room.

The Michaels family planted a church called Voyage in Bremerton, Washington, in 2009. They have created a unique and homey coffee-shop environment for Voyage and are passionate about reaching out to emerging generations.

Connect with Melissa and other home lovers through The Inspired Room (theinspiredroom.net) and use the subscribe option if you'd like to have new, free blog posts delivered to your email inbox. You can also reach Melissa at melissa@theinspiredroom.com. Follow her at Facebook.com/theinspiredroom.fans and on Instragram, Pinterest, and Twitter as theinspiredroom.

Create and share your own home love story and be inspired by stories created by others at Melissa's site homelovestories.com.

For more information on Melissa's books, including free downloads and other home and book-related resources, visit:
lovethehomeyouhave.com.

To learn more about Harvest House books and
to read sample chapters, visit our website:

www.harvesthousepublishers.com

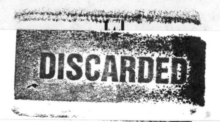